THE REVISED VERSION
EDITED FOR THE USE OF SCHOOLS

THE
BOOK OF GENESIS

XXV—L

T0381941

THE
BOOK OF GENESIS
XXV—L

BY

H. C. O. LANCHESTER, M.A.

RECTOR OF FRAMLINGHAM, SUFFOLK
FORMERLY FELLOW OF PEMBROKE COLLEGE, CAMBRIDGE

CAMBRIDGE
AT THE UNIVERSITY PRESS
1924

CAMBRIDGE
UNIVERSITY PRESS

University Printing House, Cambridge CB2 8BS, United Kingdom

Published in the United States of America by Cambridge University Press, New York

Cambridge University Press is part of the University of Cambridge.

It furthers the University's mission by disseminating knowledge in the pursuit of education, learning and research at the highest international levels of excellence.

www.cambridge.org
Information on this title: www.cambridge.org/9781107696259

© Cambridge University Press 1924

First published 1924
First paperback edition 2014

A catalogue record for this publication is available from the British Library

ISBN 978-1-107-69625-9 Paperback

Additional resources for this publication at www.cambridge.org/9781107696259

PREFACE BY THE GENERAL EDITOR
FOR THE OLD TESTAMENT

THE aim of this series of commentaries is to explain the Revised Version for young students, and at the same time to present, in a simple form, the main results of the best scholarship of the day.

The General Editor has confined himself to supervision and suggestion. The writer is, in each case, responsible for the opinions expressed and for the treatment of particular passages.

A. H. McNEILE.

DUBLIN,
March, 1923.

CONTENTS

MAP

*PALESTINE AND EGYPT

*available for download in colour from www.cambridge.org/9781107696259

INTRODUCTION

I. The Scope of the Chapters.

THE second half of Genesis begins with a postscript to
the story of Abraham, giving a list of his sons by Keturah,
and another list of the descendants of Ishmael. Between
the two is inserted a notice of the death and burial of
Abraham.

The narrative then proceeds with the history of Isaac, but
the interest is soon transferred to Esau and Jacob, and
more particularly to Jacob. After Jacob has by treachery
secured the blessing that should have been Esau's he fills
the whole stage, and his adventures on the way to Haran,
during his stay with Laban, and on his journey back to
Canaan, are told without interruption. At Hebron he rejoins
his father, now in extreme old age, and just as Isaac and
Ishmael are brought together to bury Abraham, so Esau
and Jacob join in burying Isaac. After this a chapter is
inserted dealing with the generations of Esau, and then
from xxxvii. onward the book is mainly taken up with the
story of Joseph, which is told in considerable detail. There
is one rather long interruption (Chapter xxxviii.), which
gives the story of Judah and Tamar. This seems out of
place, but it is inserted here probably because there was
no other obvious place, and the story of Joseph had only
just begun.

Joseph's history is perhaps the most vivid and arresting
of the Old Testament stories, but there is no need to enter
into details about it here. From the time that his father
sends him forth as a stripling to find his brethren till he
sees him again years after in Egypt, the excitement of the

story never flags. Many details are inserted illustrating the manners and customs of Egypt, as for example the reason for the peculiar system of land tenure, but Joseph is the hero throughout. Jacob when he arrives in Egypt comes for the moment to the front again. As head of the family he blesses Joseph's children, and is represented as uttering an oracular prophecy about the fortunes of the descendants of his several sons. With the death of Jacob and his burial in Canaan the book is almost at its close. It remains only to relate how Joseph gave charge about his own burial, and dying full of years and honour was embalmed by the Egyptians.

It will be seen from this sketch that the later chapters of Genesis are very largely taken up with the histories of two men, Jacob and Joseph. Isaac is a somewhat shadowy figure, and Esau is obviously off the main line of the story. None of the other figures come into any real prominence. From this it is clear that the compiler is concerned to trace the way in which God's promise to Abraham was gradually fulfilled in the main line of his descendants through Isaac, Jacob, and his twelve sons.

2. THE ANTIQUARIAN INTEREST.

Of the three sources (J, E, and P) from which the book of Genesis is compiled, J is specially concerned with matters of antiquarian interest, and P with the question of ethnology or the relation of different peoples to each other.

We will take the latter first.

The Hebrews were surrounded by peoples, tribes and clans which were obviously akin to them and to each other, though differing in numbers and importance, and showing traces of other strains due to intermarriage with people of other races. Questions of genealogy exercised a special fascination for the Hebrews, as was natural among a people who laid the greatest stress on pureness of descent, and traditions as to the origin of the various peoples were treasured with particular care. Broadly speaking a common ancestor was found in Abraham : the line of true descent was traced from him through Isaac, Jacob, and the twelve patriarchs : the peoples nearest to the Hebrews were derived from Esau the true son of Isaac, who should have inherited the birthright, but who spoiled the pureness of the race by marrying foreign wives : while other races, less closely connected, were regarded as descended from the patriarchs by secondary wives or concubines. Hence we get the descendants of Ishmael in xxv. 12–16, and of Keturah in xxv. 1–4. That the names in many cases refer to tribes rather than to individuals is plain from the use of the plural termination -*im* in some instances (cf. xxv. 3). That the Hebrews regarded the Aramæans of Northern Syria as specially akin to them, although they spoke a different tongue (xxxi. 47), is clear from the fact that Jacob is represented as finding wives from the daughters of Laban the Syrian.

So just as the list of nations in ch. x. gives the Hebrew idea of the inter-relation of the main races of the world, similarly the catalogues of chs. xxv. and xxxvi. attempt to explain the degrees of relationship which were thought to exist between the Hebrews and the peoples or clans that were more or less akin to them.

The antiquarian interest of J is of a different kind. He is always careful to give, sometimes quite unscientifically, the meanings and derivations of names: e.g. Jacob (xxv. 26, xxvii. 36), Edom (xxv. 30), Bethel (xxviii. 17, 19), many of the sons of Jacob (xxix. 32 ff.), Mahanaim (xxxii. 2), Peniel (xxxii. 30), Succoth (xxxiii. 17), Allon-bacuth (xxxv. 8), Perez (xxxviii. 29), Manasseh (xli. 51), Ephraim (xli. 52). He notes the curious fact that the Israelites do not eat a certain part of the leg of animals, and gives the derivation of the custom (xxxii. 32). He also emphasizes the earliness of the custom of the levirate law (xxxviii. 8). He has a special interest in Egyptian manners and customs, e.g. their exclusiveness in eating (xliii. 32), the practice of magic (xliv. 5), their system of land tenure, and the influence of the priests (xlvii. 26), their practice of embalming the bodies of the dead (l. 2, 3, 26). Broadly it may be said that his interests are human in the widest sense, and that he loses no opportunity of making his narrative more vivid by notes and explanations.

E has special information about Egypt, e.g. the custom of celebrating the king's birthday by an amnesty (xl. 20), the destructive sirocco or east wind (xli. 23), the position of a Grand Vizier (xli. 41–43). It is E too who gives actual Egyptian words and names, e.g. the river [Nile] (xli. 1), the reed grass (xli. 18), "Bow the knee" (xli. 43), Zaphenath-paneah (xli. 45). E has also a good deal to say about Jacob's stay in Syria, and his return to Canaan.

3. THE RELIGIOUS IDEAS OF THE TIME.

The picture of religious life and thought given in these chapters is of great interest. We will take first the thought of God, and His dealings with men.

According to the older tradition (J) He appears in person to men to give His commands or messages. So He appears to Isaac (xxvi. 2, 24), and to Jacob (xxviii. 13). In the later tradition (E) His commands are given by an angel (xxxi. 11), or by a dream (as to Laban, xxxi. 24), or in visions (as to Jacob, xlvi. 2). Sometimes (as in xxxi. 3, xxxv. 1), the means of communication is not specified. In two passages (xxviii. 12, xxxii. 1) the angels are represented as God's messengers. God is conceived of as intervening in various ways in the affairs of life. He is the protector (xxviii. 15, xxxi. 7), and the giver of prosperity (xxx. 27, xxxix. 3, 23), or the witness of wrong (xxxi. 50), and the punisher (xliv. 16). His overruling providence orders all things (xlv. 7, 8, l. 20). It is He who sends dreams and their interpretation (xli. 25). It is He who blesses family life and gives the blessing of children (xxv. 21, xxx. 17, 22, xxxiii. 5, xli. 52).

With regard to the ordinances of religion we find mention of the custom of visiting special sanctuaries to obtain oracles from God (xxv. 22). Altars are erected in different places to mark special events (xxvi. 25, xxxiii. 20, xxxv. 7), or sacred pillars, which are consecrated by oil poured upon them (xxviii. 18, xxxv. 14). Sacrifices are mentioned in xxxi. 54, xlvi. 1, and in xxviii. 22 Jacob makes a conditional vow to give a tithe of his substance to God. The practice of circumcision is emphasized in the story told in xxxiv. A taint of idolatry is associated with Laban's home in Haran. So when Jacob steals away on his homeward journey Rachel takes with her the teraphim or images of household gods (xxxi. 19), and Laban on discovering his loss complains that Jacob has stolen his gods (xxxi. 30). There are also "strange gods" among Jacob's household which have to be taken away before he reaches Canaan (xxxv. 2). These gods are coupled with rings (xxxv. 4), which were apparently used as amulets. Finally Joseph is presented as claiming supernatural powers of divination (xliv. 15), which he practises by means of a divining cup (xliv. 5). But this may possibly have been no more than a device to impress his brethren and test their sincerity.

4. The Religious Lessons.

One of the main interests of the second half of Genesis lies in its masterly delineation of character. The narrative centres mainly round two figures, Jacob and Joseph, and each is made to live before us.

Jacob is a complex character, astute and largely unscrupulous, yet never lacking in finer instincts, and capable of rising above himself. His life is a record of hard work and anxiety, but it is crowned with a peaceful and contented end.

The religious development of his character is of special interest. If he obtains by fraud the blessing that should have belonged to his brother, he goes far to justify that fraud by proving himself capable of higher things than Esau "the profane." Trouble and anxiety bring out the better sides of his nature, and there are two incidents which stand out as definite turning points in his life. The first is the experience at Beth-el, when in his loneliness and helplessness he is comforted by the assurance of the nearness and of the protection of God. The other is associated with Peniel on his journey back from Mesopotamia. There on the eve of his meeting once more the brother he had wronged, he is represented as agonizing in solitary prayer, until by his persistence he wins the assurance of blessing that he had sought. The two stories mark a definite progress. At Beth-el (God's house) he sees God afar off at the top of the heavenly staircase, and is assured of His care: at Peniel (God's face) he clings close to Him and receives His blessing.

Joseph's is a different type of character. He has no great faults to conquer, and he appears throughout as a simple and sunny nature which adjusts itself without much difficulty to the most varied surroundings, and emerges triumphant from every affliction. The keynote of his character lies in his unflinching adherence to God's laws, and his never failing recognition of God's guiding Providence.

So his great temptation finds no echo in his will, because he feels instinctively that to yield to it would be to sin against God. And at the end of the story his forgiveness of his brethren is full and complete because he feels that God's hand has been guiding each scene in the drama of his life. It is not hard to imagine what an influence the story of Joseph would have on the minds of the generations of Israelites who studied it. The doctrine that innocence inevitably brings material reward, which forms, for example, the theme of Ps. xxxvii, and is so strikingly illustrated in the story of Joseph is no doubt over-emphasized, but Joseph's character is one that forms no mean or unworthy ideal. His spotless integrity, his cheerful acceptance of unmerited hardship, his constant determination to do his best under all circumstances, his love for his father, and his readiness to forgive his brethren, all combine to make up the picture of a singularly lovable and attractive personality.

5. THE ISRAELITES IN EGYPT.

One of the most abiding memories of Israel as a nation was that of the years they lived in Egypt. The memory was a bitter one, and for many centuries Egypt was associated with the idea of suffering and hardship (Deut. iv. 20). Possibly the yearly recurrence of the Passover, which commemorated their deliverance from "bondage," was partly responsible for this.

The book of Genesis has nothing to say about the Egyptian oppression. But it tells the story of how the ancestors of the Hebrew race came to settle in Egypt as a little band of about 70 persons, and it would be interesting if we could date this event and fit it into the scheme of Egyptian history as we know it. Unfortunately this is a matter of considerable uncertainty. We should be in a better position if we knew for certain the date of the Exodus, for in Exod. xii. 40 we find the total length of the Israelites' sojourn in Egypt given as 430 years, and this does not differ widely from the 400 years given in Stephen's speech in Acts vii. 6. In 1 Kings vi. 1, we seem to have a definite date for the Exodus, 480 years before the building of Solomon's Temple which we may put at about 966, giving 1446 for the date of the Exodus, and about 1876 B.C. for the entry of Jacob and his family into Egypt. In 1446 Amenhotep II was king of Egypt. Many scholars however find this date too early in view of the subsequent history of the Israelites, and would prefer to date the Exodus in the reign of Merenptah who came to the throne in 1225 B.C. We have then two possible dates for Joseph, *c.* 1876 B.C. and *c.* 1635 B.C., and it is impossible to decide authoritatively between them.

There is one event in Egyptian history about this time that has a real bearing on the whole question. At a date probably about 1780 B.C., but possibly before that, a foreign race known as the Hyksos held sway in Egypt. Manetho, the Egyptian historian, says that their name means Shepherd Kings, and he may very likely be right. He also says that they made their capital at Avaris in the Delta, and this Prof. Peet identifies with good reason with Pelusium situated at the mouth of the most easterly branch of the Nile, just north of the land of Goshen. The Hyksos appear to have been a Semitic race, and there is a good deal to be said for the view that the Hebrews entered Egypt while they were in power, and that the kindness of the Pharaoh to Jacob and his family was partly due to the fact that they were both of Semitic stock. The Hyksos were expelled from Egypt about 1580 B.C., and this would account for the fact that later on "a new king arose which knew not Joseph" (Exod. i. 8), who oppressed the Hebrews.

But if a Hyksos king was on the throne when Jacob and his family came into Egypt, the note in Gen. xlvi. 34, to the effect that "every shepherd is an abomination to the Egyptians" would seem to be out of place and to reflect the spirit of a later age which looked back with loathing to the dominion of the Shepherd Kings.

It must be remembered that there was a constant tendency for nomads from Palestine and the surrounding countries to try to make their way into the fertile and well tilled plains of Egypt. When the Egyptian government was strong the frontier was closely guarded, but in times of disorganization the strangers gained a foothold. So a migration of 70 persons from Canaan to Egypt would not attract much notice, especially if they settled in that part of the land which immediately adjoined the frontier.

6. THE STORY OF JOSEPH AS A DRAMA.

It may be that the story of Joseph is literal history. It moves naturally from stage to stage, and there is nothing inherently impossible or even improbable in the idea that a Hebrew slave should by his perseverance and ability rise to the position of Grand Vizier, second only to the king. But it may also be dramatized history in the same kind of way as Shakespeare's histories are. At any rate the man who put the story together has shown the most consummate dramatic skill.

Aristotle has noted that there are two elements which are proper to a tragedy. One is the "reversal of fortune" which brings a man from prosperity to ruin or *vice versa*. The other is the "recognition," the "change from ignorance to knowledge, producing love or hatred between the persons destined by the poet for good or bad fortune." Each plays an important part in the story of Joseph. He experiences three reversals of fortune, two from good to bad when from being his father's favourite son he is sold as a slave into a distant land, and again when from his rising prospects in Potiphar's house he is unjustly put into prison. The third "reversal" is of the happier kind, when he is taken from prison to be the second ruler in the land. Of "recognitions" there are two: one a false one when

Jacob recognizes the coat of his son whom he imagines to have been slain, and one a true one when Joseph makes himself known to his brethren. It would probably be no exaggeration to say that in all literature there is no finer example of "recognition" than this, and it comes at a most dramatic moment when the sympathy of the reader has been strongly moved by the noble appeal of Judah. It is so extraordinarily fine as literature that it becomes a matter of comparatively minor importance whether it is literally true or not. At any rate its main value lies not so much in its historical accuracy as in the great lessons which it is designed to bring out and illustrate.

7. ANALYSIS.

THE FIRST BOOK OF MOSES,

COMMONLY CALLED

GENESIS

xxv. 1–6. *Abraham's sons by Keturah.*

And Abraham took another wife, and her name was 25
Keturah. And she bare him Zimran, and Jokshan, and 2
Medan, and Midian, and Ishbak, and Shuah. And Jok- 3
shan begat Sheba, and Dedan. And the sons of Dedan
were Asshurim, and Letushim, and Leummim. And the 4
sons of Midian; Ephah, and Epher, and Hanoch, and
Abida, and Eldaah. All these were the children of Keturah. And Abraham gave all that he had unto Isaac. 5
But unto the sons of the concubines, which Abraham had, 6
Abraham gave gifts; and he sent them away from Isaac
his son, while he yet lived, eastward, unto the east country.

7–11. *Death and burial of Abraham.*

And these are the days of the years of Abraham's life which 7
he lived, an hundred threescore and fifteen years. And 8

---

xxv. 1–6. The names of the sons represent Arab tribes, and
the purpose of the list is apparently to explain the kinship of these
tribes to the Israelites, and at the same time to point out their
inferiority as members of a secondary branch of the family.

1. Keturah. The word means 'incense,' and Arabia was famous for incense.

2. Shuah: the country of Bildad, the Shuhite, one of the three
friends of Job.

3. Asshurim. The plural termination *-im* shews that we are not
dealing with individuals here, but tribes. Asshur stands for Assyria, but these Asshurim were probably an Arabian tribe, not the
Assyrians.

6. the concubines: i.e. Hagar and Keturah.

Abraham gave up the ghost, and died in a good old age, an old man, and full *of years*; and was gathered to his
9 people. And Isaac and Ishmael his sons buried him in the cave of Machpelah, in the field of Ephron the son
10 of Zohar the Hittite, which is before Mamre; the field which Abraham purchased of the children of Heth: there
11 was Abraham buried, and Sarah his wife. And it came to pass after the death of Abraham, that God blessed Isaac his son; and Isaac dwelt by Beer-lahai-roi.

12-18. *The descendants of Ishmael.*

12   Now these are the generations of Ishmael, Abraham's son, whom Hagar the Egyptian, Sarah's handmaid, bare unto
13 Abraham: and these are the names of the sons of Ishmael, by their names, according to their generations: the firstborn of Ishmael, Nebaioth; and Kedar, and Adbeel, and Mibsam,
14 / 15 and Mishma, and Dumah, and Massa; Hadad, and Tema,
16 Jetur, Naphish, and Kedemah; these are the sons of Ishmael, and these are their names, by their villages, and by their encampments; twelve princes according to their
17 nations. And these are the years of the life of Ishmael,

---

8. was gathered to his people. A common phrase for death, cf. *v.* 17, xxxv. 29, xlix. 29, etc.

9. Isaac and Ishmael. Here only are they found together since their childhood. P, from which source these verses are taken, has no mention of the expulsion of Ishmael.

10. Abraham...and Sarah his wife. There was room for both in Machpelah, the "double" cave of xxiii. 9.

12-18. The formal style of these verses, and the character-istic language shew that they came from P. The writer disposes of the descendants of Ishmael before he goes on to the main stream of the history in Isaac, in much the same way as in xxxvi. he disposes of the descendants of Esau before proceeding to the story of Joseph.

13. Nebaioth. A district celebrated for its rams, cf. Isa. lx. 7.
Kedar: also mentioned in Isa. lx. 7 as a sheep country, and elsewhere as a nomad tribe, cf. Ps. cxx. 5; Song of Songs i. 5.

16. encampments: i.e. collections of huts, cf. Ps. lxix. 25.

an hundred and thirty and seven years: and he gave up the ghost and died; and was gathered unto his people. And they dwelt from Havilah unto Shur that is before 18 Egypt, as thou goest toward Assyria: he abode in the presence of all his brethren.

19–34. *Birth of Esau and Jacob. Jacob buys the birthright.*

And these are the generations of Isaac, Abraham's son: 19 Abraham begat Isaac: and Isaac was forty years old when 20 he took Rebekah, the daughter of Bethuel the Syrian of Paddan-aram, the sister of Laban the Syrian, to be his wife. And Isaac intreated the LORD for his wife, because 21 she was barren: and the LORD was intreated of him, and Rebekah his wife conceived. And the children struggled 22 together within her; and she said, If it be so, wherefore do I live? And she went to inquire of the LORD. And the 23 LORD said unto her,

---

18. from Havilah unto Shur. For Havilah cf. ii. 11, and for Shur xvi. 7.

toward Assyria. There seems no point in the mention of Assyria, and perhaps we should connect the word with the Asshurim mentioned in *v.* 3, and understand it to refer to some region in the Arabian desert.

20. Paddan-aram, lit. 'field of Syria,' is P's name for Mesopotamia. J has regularly *Aram naharaim,* 'Syria of the two rivers.'

21. was intreated: i.e. granted the entreaty.

22. the children struggled: this struggle even before birth serves to typify the age-long enmity between Israel and Edom, cf. Ps. cxxxvii. 7.

to inquire of the LORD. It is not stated how this was accomplished. Probably she went to some place such as Beer-sheba which was regarded as a sanctuary of God.

23. The answer of God is given in the form of Hebrew poetry, one half of each verse balancing the other. It points forward to the enmity between Israel and Edom, and the superiority of Israel the younger nation.

> Two nations are in thy womb,
> And two peoples shall be separated even from thy
> bowels :
> And the one people shall be stronger than the other
> people ;
> And the elder shall serve the younger.

24 And when her days to be delivered were fulfilled, behold,
25 there were twins in her womb. And the first came forth
red, all over like an hairy garment; and they called his
26 name Esau. And after that came forth his brother, and
his hand had hold on Esau's heel ; and his name was called
Jacob : and Isaac was threescore years old when she bare
27 them. And the boys grew : and Esau was a cunning
hunter, a man of the field ; and Jacob was a plain man,
28 dwelling in tents. Now Isaac loved Esau, because he did
29 eat of his venison : and Rebekah loved Jacob. And Jacob
sod pottage : and Esau came in from the field, and he was
30 faint : and Esau said to Jacob, Feed me, I pray thee, with
that same red *pottage* ; for I am faint : therefore was his
31 name called Edom. And Jacob said, Sell me this day thy

---

25. red: referring to the name Edom = 'ruddy.'

like an hairy garment: a characteristic mentioned again in
xxvii. 11. The name Esau probably means 'hairy.'

26. had hold on Esau's heel. The action was in keeping with
Jacob's name (which is from the same root letters as the word
for 'heel'), and with his character as supplanter : cf. Hos. xii. 3.

27. a plain man : lit. 'perfect,' 'upright,' which seems a strange
epithet to apply to Jacob as a young man. The idea is 'quiet'
or 'steady.'

29. sod : a rather archaic past tense of seethe = 'boil.' German
'sieden,' 'gesotten.' For seethe cf. Deut. xiv. 21 ; 2 Kings iv.
38 etc. The past part. is sodden, cf. Exod. xii. 9 etc.

30. red *pottage*. The noun does not appear in the Hebrew.
The emphasis is on 'red' which is the same root as Edom. Possibly Esau, hungry as he is, only notices that the food is red : or
'red' may have been the term for a particular kind of pottage, in
the same kind of way as we speak of *blanc mange*.

31. Sell me...thy birthright. Jacob in his early life is a man

birthright. And Esau said, Behold, I am at the point to 32
die : and what profit shall the birthright do to me? And 33
Jacob said, Swear to me this day ; and he sware unto him :
and he sold his birthright unto Jacob. And Jacob gave 34
Esau bread and pottage of lentils ; and he did eat and
drink, and rose up, and went his way : so Esau despised
his birthright.

xxvi. 1–33. *Isaac's life in Philistia.*

And there was a famine in the land, beside the first **26**
famine that was in the days of Abraham. And Isaac went
unto Abimelech king of the Philistines unto Gerar. And 2
the LORD appeared unto him, and said, Go not down into
Egypt ; dwell in the land which I shall tell thee of : sojourn 3

---

who is always driving hard bargains. But in the O.T. he is not
blamed for this. Contrast John i. 47.

32. what profit shall the birthright do to me? Esau is the
typical 'profane man' (Hebr. xii. 16), who for present gain will
barter away without a thought God's promised blessings. His
carelessness as regards higher things is well brought out in the
words 'he did eat, and drink, and rose up, and went his way.'

xxvi. 1–33. Isaac's history, in contrast to that of Abraham
and Jacob, is a somewhat colourless one. The story of how he
disowned his wife may possibly be a different version of a tale
that had already been told of Abraham in xx. (cf. also xii. 11–20),
and the rest of the chapter is taken up with disputes as to the
ownership of wells.

1. beside the first famine : i.e. that mentioned in xii. 10.
Famines appear to recur at more or less regular intervals.

Abimelech. The same name appears as belonging to the king
of Gerar in xx. 2, but as this incident was some 80 years previous,
they can hardly refer to the same man. Possibly it was a generic
name for the kings of Gerar as Pharaoh for the kings of Egypt,
and possibly Candace for the queens of Ethiopia. Abimelech
means '(the god) Melek is my father.'

Philistines. Strictly speaking the Philistines had not yet in-
vaded Palestine, so the mention of them here is an anachronism.
Although they disappeared from history so long ago their name
is still preserved in 'Palestine.'

2. Go not down into Egypt. Egypt was usually the place of
refuge in a time of famine, cf. xiii. 10, xli. 57.

in this land, and I will be with thee, and will bless thee;
for unto thee, and unto thy seed, I will give all these lands,
and I will establish the oath which I sware unto Abraham
4 thy father; and I will multiply thy seed as the stars of
heaven, and will give unto thy seed all these lands; and
in thy seed shall all the nations of the earth be blessed;
5 because that Abraham obeyed my voice, and kept my
6 charge, my commandments, my statutes, and my laws. And
7 Isaac dwelt in Gerar: and the men of the place asked
him of his wife; and he said, She is my sister: for he
feared to say, My wife; lest, *said he*, the men of the place
should kill me for Rebekah: because she was fair to look
8 upon. And it came to pass, when he had been there a
long time, that Abimelech king of the Philistines looked
out at a window, and saw, and, behold, Isaac was sporting
9 with Rebekah his wife. And Abimelech called Isaac, and
said, Behold, of a surety she is thy wife: and how saidst
thou, She is my sister? And Isaac said unto him, Because
10 I said, Lest I die for her. And Abimelech said, What is
this thou hast done unto us? one of the people might lightly
have lien with thy wife, and thou shouldest have brought
11 guiltiness upon us. And Abimelech charged all the people,
saying, He that toucheth this man or his wife shall surely

---

3. the oath: cf. xxii. 16-18.

5. my charge...my laws. This piling up of similar words is a
marked characteristic of the style of Deuteronomy.

7. should kill me. The standard of morality is to be noticed.
Apparently adultery was reckoned as a grave offence, and murder
as a light one.

8. looked out at a window: i.e. an open casement, cf. Judg.
v. 28: 2 Sam. vi. 16.

sporting. The same Hebrew word is used in a different sense in
xxi. 9, and in each case there is a play on words with the name
Isaac, which comes from the same root.

10. lightly: i.e. easily, readily, cf. Mark ix. 39.

upon us. The misdeed of one would have brought guilt on the
people. Cf. 2 Sam. xxiv. 17.

be put to death. And Isaac sowed in that land, and found 12
n the same year an hundredfold: and the Lord blessed
him. And the man waxed great, and grew more and more 13
until he became very great: and he had possessions of 14
flocks, and possessions of herds, and a great household:
and the Philistines envied him. Now all the wells which 15
his father's servants had digged in the days of Abraham
his father, the Philistines had stopped them, and filled
them with earth. And Abimelech said unto Isaac, Go 16
from us; for thou art much mightier than we. And Isaac 17
departed thence, and encamped in the valley of Gerar,
and dwelt there. And Isaac digged again the wells of 18
water, which they had digged in the days of Abraham his
father; for the Philistines had stopped them after the death
of Abraham: and he called their names after the names
by which his father had called them. And Isaac's servants 19
digged in the valley, and found there a well of springing
water. And the herdmen of Gerar strove with Isaac's 20
herdmen, saying, The water is ours: and he called the
name of the well Esek; because they contended with him.
And they digged another well, and they strove for that 21
also: and he called the name of it Sitnah. And he re- 22

---

12. sowed. The first mention of raising crops. The plains of
Philistia have always been noted for their corn.

an hundredfold. The Hebrew word for 'fold' never occurs
again in this sense. Some of the versions render it 'barley.'
For the hundredfold increase, cf. Matt. xiii. 8.

14. household: i.e. retinue of slaves, cf. Job i. 3.

15. the Philistines had stopped them: apparently with a
view to driving Isaac and his followers from their land. Throughout this story the Philistines are always the aggressors, and Isaac
is the peacemaker; cf. xxi. 25 ff.

17. the valley of Gerar. The Hebrew word for 'valley' means
wady or water-course, often dry in summer.

19. springing water: i.e. running. Such a well would be
specially valuable.

21. Sitnah: i.e. Enmity; the same root as (the) *Satan.* Pos-

moved from thence, and digged another well; and for that
they strove not: and he called the name of it Rehoboth;
and he said, For now the LORD hath made room for us,
23 and we shall be fruitful in the land. And he went up from
24 thence to Beer-sheba. And the LORD appeared unto him
the same night, and said, I am the God of Abraham thy
father: fear not, for I am with thee, and will bless thee,
and multiply thy seed for my servant Abraham's sake.
25 And he builded an altar there, and called upon the name
of the LORD, and pitched his tent there: and there Isaac's
26 servants digged a well. Then Abimelech went to him
from Gerar, and Ahuzzath his friend, and Phicol the cap-
27 tain of his host. And Isaac said unto them, Wherefore
are ye come unto me, seeing ye hate me, and have sent
28 me away from you? And they said, We saw plainly that
the LORD was with thee: and we said, Let there now be
an oath betwixt us, even betwixt us and thee, and let us
29 make a covenant with thee; that thou wilt do us no hurt,
as we have not touched thee, and as we have done unto
thee nothing but good, and have sent thee away in peace:
30 thou art now the blessed of the LORD. And he made
31 them a feast, and they did eat and drink. And they rose
up betimes in the morning, and sware one to another: and

---

sibly the well is to be identified with the wady Sutain N. of
Ruḥaibeh (Rehoboth).

24. appeared unto him. Beer-sheba was regarded as a holy
place where God was specially near.

25. builded an altar: to mark his thankfulness for God's
promise, cf. xii. 7, xxxv. 7.

26. his friend. Probably a Court title. Cf. 2 Sam. xv. 37.

Phicol: cf. xxi. 22.

The mission of Abimelech and his officers is a testimony to the
growing importance of Isaac. Before this they sent him away
(*v.* 16). Now they come with a proposal of alliance.

30. they did eat and drink. Part of the ceremony of making
a covenant consisted of a common meal, cf. xxxi. 54.

Isaac sent them away, and they departed from him in peace. And it came to pass the same day, that Isaac's servants came, and told him concerning the well which they had digged, and said unto him, We have found water. And he called it Shibah: therefore the name of the city is Beer-sheba unto this day. 32 33

34, 35. *Esau's Hittite wives.*

And when Esau was forty years old he took to wife Judith the daughter of Beeri the Hittite, and Basemath the daughter of Elon the Hittite: and they were a grief of mind unto Isaac and to Rebekah. 34 35

xxvii. 1–45. *Jacob gains by craft his father's blessing.*

And it came to pass, that when Isaac was old, and his eyes were dim, so that he could not see, he called Esau his elder son, and said unto him, My son: and he said unto him, Here am I. And he said, Behold now, I am old, I know not the day of my death. Now therefore take, I pray thee, thy weapons, thy quiver and thy bow, and go out to the field, and take me venison; and make me **27** 2 3 4

---

33. Shibah. A rare form of the word meaning 'oath.' For the other derivation of Beer-sheba (= well of seven) cf. xxi. 31.

34. Judith: the word means 'Jewess' and it is curious to find it as the name of a Hittite woman. For the presence of Hittites cf. xxiii. 3.

35. a grief of mind : i.e. as contaminating the purity of the stock.

xxvii. 1–45. The story is told with all the vividness and pathos of which J is such a master. If we are surprised that nothing is said in condemnation of Jacob's action, we must remember (*a*) that the standard of truth and honesty was not always very high in primitive times, (*b*) that usually in the O.T. the reader is left to draw for himself the moral of a story, (*c*) that the subsequent history shews how under God's hand both Rebekah and Jacob were punished for their deceit.

1. his eyes were dim. A common mark of old age. Cf. 1 Kings xiv. 4 and contrast Deut. xxxiv. 7.

savoury meat, such as I love, and bring it to me, that I
5 may eat; that my soul may bless thee before I die. And
Rebekah heard when Isaac spake to Esau his son. And
Esau went to the field to hunt for venison, and to bring it.
6 And Rebekah spake unto Jacob her son, saying, Behold,
I heard thy father speak unto Esau thy brother, saying,
7 Bring me venison, and make me savoury meat, that I may
eat, and bless thee before the LORD before my death.
8 Now therefore, my son, obey my voice according to that
9 which I command thee. Go now to the flock, and fetch
me from thence two good kids of the goats; and I will
make them savoury meat for thy father, such as he loveth:
10 and thou shalt bring it to thy father, that he may eat, so
11 that he may bless thee before his death. And Jacob said to
Rebekah his mother, Behold, Esau my brother is a hairy
12 man, and I am a smooth man. My father peradventure
will feel me, and I shall seem to him as a deceiver; and
13 I shall bring a curse upon me, and not a blessing. And
his mother said unto him, Upon me be thy curse, my son:
14 only obey my voice, and go fetch me them. And he went,
and fetched, and brought them to his mother: and his
15 mother made savoury meat, such as his father loved. And
Rebekah took the goodly raiment of Esau her elder son,

---

4. that I may eat. Isaac implies that when his heart is
strengthened by the food his son has brought, he will be the better
able to pronounce a fitting blessing 'before the Lord,' i.e. in God's
name.

11. a hairy man: cf. xxv. 25. Jacob raises no objection on
moral grounds to his mother's plan, but he cautiously suggests
difficulties that must be smoothed away. His cunning seems
to have been inherited from his mother, but perhaps his spiritual
capacities were also.

13. Upon me be thy curse: i.e. any curse that Isaac may in-
voke upon thee. Cf. Matt. xxvii. 25.

15. the goodly raiment: i.e. the clothes worn at festivals and
on special occasions. It is a touch of life that causes the narrator
to represent Rebekah as careful to send Jacob fittingly dressed

which were with her in the house, and put them upon
Jacob her younger son: and she put the skins of the kids 16
of the goats upon his hands, and upon the smooth of his
neck: and she gave the savoury meat and the bread, 17
which she had prepared, into the hand of her son Jacob.
And he came unto his father, and said, My father: and 18
he said, Here am I; who art thou, my son? And Jacob 19
said unto his father, I am Esau thy firstborn; I have done
according as thou badest me: arise, I pray thee, sit and
eat of my venison, that thy soul may bless me. And Isaac 20
said unto his son, How is it that thou hast found it so
quickly, my son? And he said, Because the LORD thy
God sent me good speed. And Isaac said unto Jacob, 21
Come near, I pray thee, that I may feel thee, my son,
whether thou be my very son Esau or not. And Jacob 22
went near unto Isaac his father; and he felt him, and said,
The voice is Jacob's voice, but the hands are the hands of
Esau. And he discerned him not, because his hands were 23
hairy, as his brother Esau's hands: so he blessed him.
And he said, Art thou my very son Esau? And he said, 24
I am. And he said, Bring it near to me, and I will eat of 25
my son's venison, that my soul may bless thee. And he
brought it near to him, and he did eat: and he brought
him wine, and he drank. And his father Isaac said unto 26
him, Come near now, and kiss me, my son. And he came 27

---

to receive the blessing, and Esau 'the profane man' as apparently
caring nothing for such a detail.

20. Because the LORD thy God sent me good speed. The narrator perhaps intends to illustrate Jacob's quick-wittedness by this
his reply, but to our minds it is taking God's name in vain.

21. that I may feel thee. A blind man sees very largely by
sense of touch.

22. The voice is Jacob's voice. Apparently Rebekah had over-
looked the detail of the different voices, and it went near to
wreck the whole scheme.

near, and kissed him: and he smelled the smell of his
raiment, and blessed him, and said,

> See, the smell of my son
> Is as the smell of a field which the LORD hath blessed:

28   And God give thee of the dew of heaven,
> And of the fatness of the earth,
> And plenty of corn and wine:

29   Let peoples serve thee,
> And nations bow down to thee:
> Be lord over thy brethren,
> And let thy mother's sons bow down to thee:
> Cursed be every one that curseth thee,
> And blessed be every one that blesseth thee.

30 And it came to pass, as soon as Isaac had made an end
of blessing Jacob, and Jacob was yet scarce gone out from
the presence of Isaac his father, that Esau his brother

31 came in from his hunting. And he also made savoury
meat, and brought it unto his father; and he said unto his
father, Let my father arise, and eat of his son's venison,

32 that thy soul may bless me. And Isaac his father said

---

28. The blessing which is put into poetical form promises three
things, (i) a fruitful land, (ii) national greatness, (iii) influence for
good or evil on others.

of the dew of heaven. Palestine depends largely on the dew
for its fertility. Cf. Ps. cxxxiii. 3; Isa. xviii. 4; Hos. xiv. 5.

29. Be lord over thy brethren: looking forward to the conquest of Edom. Cf. the oracle given to Rebekah in xxv. 23.

30. came in from his hunting. Not into his father's presence,
but to the place where he would cook the venison. Notice that
he does not ask his mother to help him. He will do everything
himself to prepare for his father's solemn meal.

31. he also made: A.V. 'he also had made,' which is grammati-
cally incorrect, conveys the impression that Esau followed immediately upon Jacob's exit. But some time must have elapsed while
he was cooking the meat.

Let my father arise. Comparing Esau's words with those of
Jacob in *v.* 19 we seem to detect a strain of deeper affection in
Esau for his father.

unto him, Who art thou? And he said, I am thy son, thy
firstborn, Esau. And Isaac trembled very exceedingly, 33
and said, Who then is he that hath taken venison, and
brought it me, and I have eaten of all before thou camest,
and have blessed him? yea, *and* he shall be blessed. When 34
Esau heard the words of his father, he cried with an ex-
ceeding great and bitter cry, and said unto his father,
Bless me, even me also, O my father. And he said, Thy 35
brother came with guile, and hath taken away thy blessing.
And he said, Is not he rightly named Jacob? for he hath 36
supplanted me these two times: he took away my birthright; and, behold, now he hath taken away my blessing.
And he said, Hast thou not reserved a blessing for me?
And Isaac answered and said unto Esau, Behold, I have 37
made him thy lord, and all his brethren have I given to
him for servants; and with corn and wine have I sustained
him: and what then shall I do for thee, my son? And 38
Esau said unto his father, Hast thou but one blessing, my
father? bless me, even me also, O my father. And Esau lifted
up his voice, and wept. And Isaac his father answered 39
and said unto him,

> Behold, of the fatness of the earth shall be thy dwell-
> ing,
> And of the dew of heaven from above;

---

34. Bless me, even me also. Esau at once recognizes that the
blessing once spoken is irrevocable, but he begs for some crumbs
of blessing for himself. The pathos is very marked, and Esau's
hopes grow less and less. Cf. *vv.* 36, 38.

36. he hath supplanted me: a bittter play on the name Jacob.
See note on xxv. 26.

39. of the fatness of the earth: R.V. marg. *away from.*
Thus two opposite meanings can be obtained from the Hebrew
preposition. If R.V. text is right, the blessing describes the
future territory and fortunes of Edom. The country of Edom was
by no means sterile or unfruitful. Mal. i. 3 however seems to
support the reading of R.V. marg., and it is on the whole more
probable.

40   And by thy sword shalt thou live, and thou shalt serve
         thy brother;
       And it shall come to pass when thou shalt break
         loose,
       That thou shalt shake his yoke from off thy neck.

41 And Esau hated Jacob because of the blessing wherewith
   his father blessed him: and Esau said in his heart, The
   days of mourning for my father are at hand; then will
42 I slay my brother Jacob. And the words of Esau her elder
   son were told to Rebekah; and she sent and called Jacob
   her younger son, and said unto him, Behold, thy brother
   Esau, as touching thee, doth comfort himself, *purposing*
43 to kill thee. Now therefore, my son, obey my voice; and
44 arise, flee thou to Laban my brother to Haran; and tarry
   with him a few days, until thy brother's fury turn away;
45 until thy brother's anger turn away from thee, and he
   forget that which thou hast done to him: then I will send,

---

40. by thy sword shalt thou live. The Edomites were always
a turbulent race, and depended less on the fertility of their land
than on the success of plundering expeditions.

shalt serve thy brother. David subdued the Edomites (2 Sam.
viii. 14), and they remained subject to Judah till the reigns of
Jehoram (2 Kings viii. 20-22) and Ahaz (2 Kings xvi. 6).

break loose. The verb is rare (Ps. viii. 3; Jer. ii. 31; Hos.
xii. 1) and the meaning uncertain. Perhaps = 'become restless'
or 'strive.' Historically this might be said to have been fulfilled
when Hadad the Edomite began to be an adversary to Solomon,
1 Kings xi. 14.

41. said in his heart. Yet his words were reported to
Rebekah. Perhaps his whole demeanour betrayed his purpose.

days of mourning. Possibly these would offer special oppor-
tunities for his dark deed. Or it may be that he hesitated to
commit it while his father was alive, lest he should cause him grief.

43. obey my voice: cf. *vv.* 8, 13. Throughout this story
Rebekah is the chief actor. She is one of the masterful women of
the O.T.

Laban my brother: cf. xxiv. 29.

Haran: apparently the same as 'the city of Nahor' in xxiv. 10.

44. a few days. These lengthened out to over 20 years.

and fetch thee from thence : why should I be bereaved of
you both in one day?

> xxvii. 46–xxviii. 9. *Jacob is sent out by his father and
> mother to Haran to obtain a wife.*

And Rebekah said to Isaac, I am weary of my life 46
because of the daughters of Heth : if Jacob take a wife of
the daughters of Heth, such as these, of the daughters of
the land, what good shall my life do me? And Isaac called **28**
Jacob, and blessed him, and charged him, and said unto
him, Thou shalt not take a wife of the daughters of Canaan.
Arise, go to Paddan-aram, to the house of Bethuel thy 2
mother's father ; and take thee a wife from thence of the
daughters of Laban thy mother's brother.   And God 3
Almighty bless thee, and make thee fruitful, and multiply
thee, that thou mayest be a company of peoples ; and give 4
thee the blessing of Abraham, to thee, and to thy seed
with thee ; that thou mayest inherit the land of thy
sojournings, which God gave unto Abraham. And Isaac 5
sent away Jacob : and he went to Paddan-aram unto
Laban, son of Bethuel the Syrian, the brother of Rebekah

---

45. bereaved of you both. Esau would pay the penalty with
his life at the hands of the 'avenger of blood.'

xxvii. 46–xxviii. 9. In this section there is no reference to
Jacob having to flee from his brother's wrath. It comes from the
later source, P, in which Mesopotamia is regularly called Paddan-
aram (xxviii. 2). It will be noticed that Jacob, not Esau, is treated
by Isaac as the heir of this promise.

46. the daughters of Heth : i.e. Esau's two Hittite wives
whose names are given in xxvi. 34.

what good shall my life do me? Cf. xxv. 22. There is a
strain of recklessness in Rebekah's manner of speech.

xxviii. 3. God Almighty : Hebr. *El Shaddai*. In P. the patri-
archal name for God, cf. xvii. 1. The blessing is in its language
thoroughly characteristic of P. Contrast xxvii. 27–29.

5. he went to Paddan-aram. P. merely relates the bare fact.
The next chapter, which depicts so vividly an incident of the
journey, comes from J.

6 Jacob's and Esau's mother. Now Esau saw that Isaac
  had blessed Jacob and sent him away to Paddan-aram, to
  take him a wife from thence; and that as he blessed him
  he gave him a charge, saying, Thou shalt not take a wife
7 of the daughters of Canaan; and that Jacob obeyed his
  father and his mother, and was gone to Paddan-aram:
8 and Esau saw that the daughters of Canaan pleased not
9 Isaac his father; and Esau went unto Ishmael, and took
  unto the wives which he had Mahalath the daughter of
  Ishmael Abraham's son, the sister of Nebaioth, to be his
  wife.

xxviii. 10–22. *Jacob's dream.*

0 And Jacob went out from Beer-sheba, and went toward
1 Haran. And he lighted upon a certain place, and tarried
  there all night, because the sun was set; and he took one
  of the stones of the place, and put it under his head, and
2 lay down in that place to sleep. And he dreamed, and behold a ladder set up on the earth, and the top of it reached
  to heaven: and behold the angels of God ascending and

---

9. Esau went unto Ishmael. For all his faults Esau is always
trying to please his father: so he too takes a kinswoman for his
wife.

Mahalath...the sister of Nebaioth. In xxxvi. 3 her name is
given as Basemath.

10–22. The narrative is picked up from xxvii. 45.

10. from Beer-sheba. Isaac had apparently been dwelling
there for many years, cf. xxvi. 23.

11. one of the stones of the place. Stanley (*Sinai and Palestine*, p. 219) notes that the valley near Beth-el (modern Beitin)
is 'covered, as with grave stones, by large sheets of bare rock,
some few standing up here and there like cromlechs' (quoted
by Driver). Hence the 'ladder' in the next verse must be understood rather as a stone staircase wide enough for people to pass
on it. It has been compared to the terraces leading up to a
Babylonian or Assyrian temple.

12. the angels of God. In Genesis the phrase, in the plural,
is found elsewhere only in xxxii. 1, 2. The angels are represented
as 'king's messengers' busily engaged in carrying God's messages

descending on it. And, behold, the LORD stood above it, and 13
said, I am the LORD, the God of Abraham thy father, and
the God of Isaac: the land whereon thou liest, to thee will
I give it, and to thy seed; and thy seed shall be as the 14
dust of the earth, and thou shalt spread abroad to the west
and to the east, and to the north, and to the south: and
in thee and in thy seed shall all the families of the earth
be blessed. And, behold, I am with thee, and will keep thee 15
whithersoever thou goest, and will bring thee again into
this land; for I will not leave thee, until I have done that
which I have spoken to thee of. And Jacob awaked out 16
of his sleep, and he said, Surely the LORD is in this place;
and I knew it not. And he was afraid, and said, How 17
dreadful is this place! this is none other but the house of
God, and this is the gate of heaven. And Jacob rose up 18
early in the morning, and took the stone that he had put
under his head, and set it up for a pillar, and poured oil

---

to earth and returning with the answers. But to Jacob God
Himself speaks, and he is filled with awe and wonder. Compare
our Lord's allusion to this scene in John i. 51.

15. I am with thee. The blessing is very complete, compris-
ing (i) constant protection, (ii) safe return, (iii) the sure fulfilment
of all God's promises.

17. How dreadful is this place! Rather 'awe-inspiring.' The
sight of God was popularly supposed to bring death, cf. Judg.
vi. 22 f., xiii. 21 f.

the house of God: hence the name Beth-el.

the gate of heaven: i.e. the spot where the heavenly staircase,
invisible except in dream, met the earth. Jacob seems to have
regarded the place as the point of actual communication between
heaven and earth. It may be noticed that Babel or Babylon also
means 'the gate of God' or 'of the gods.'

18. for a pillar. One of the features of the ancient Canaanite
worship which the Israelites took over was the stone pillar set up
beside the altar and technically known as the *maṣṣēbah*. Such
are condemned in Deut. xvi. 22. For another 'pillar' set up by
Jacob and consecrated in like manner cf. xxxv. 14.

poured oil: i.e. to consecrate it. It is not strange that Jacob's
scanty luggage should have included a little oil, for it is found

19 upon the top of it. And he called the name of that place
   Beth-el: but the name of the city was Luz at the first.
20 And Jacob vowed a vow, saying, If God will be with me,
   and will keep me in this way that I go, and will give me bread
21 to eat, and raiment to put on, so that I come again to my
   father's house in peace, then shall the LORD be my God,
22 and this stone, which I have set up for a pillar, shall be
   God's house: and of all that thou shalt give me I will
   surely give the tenth unto thee.

xxix. 1–14. *Jacob arrives at Laban's house.*

29 Then Jacob went on his journey, and came to the land
 2 of the children of the east. And he looked, and behold a
   well in the field, and, lo, three flocks of sheep lying there
   by it; for out of that well they watered the flocks: and
 3 the stone upon the well's mouth was great. And thither
   were all the flocks gathered: and they rolled the stone

---

almost a necessity in the East to counteract the effect of the sun
on the skin.

19. the name of the city was Luz. From Josh. xvi. 2 we
learn that Luz was distinct from Beth-el. Obviously the place of
Jacob's dream was not a city, though Beth-el afterwards over-
shadowed Luz.

20. vowed a vow : the first recorded instance of a practice that
later became very common, cf. Numb. xxi. 2, Judg. xi. 30, etc.

22. this stone...shall be God's house. Jacob promises to main-
tain the service of God at that spot.

give the tenth unto thee. In xiv. 20 Abraham pays tithe to
Melchizedek, but this and Amos iv. 2 (also referring to Beth-el)
are the only instances of tithe-paying before the days of Deuteronomy.

xxix. 1. went on his journey: lit. 'lifted his feet,' a vivid
phrase expressing the renewed hope with which he continued his
journey.

children of the east: a vague phrase often applied to the
people living east of Palestine, cf. Judg. vi. 3, vii. 12, viii. 10, etc.
Here of the inhabitants of Haran.

2. they watered the flocks. The subject is as often indefinite.
We should more naturally use the passive 'the flocks were
watered.'

from the well's mouth, and watered the sheep, and put the stone again upon the well's mouth in its place. And Jacob 4 said unto them, My brethren, whence be ye? And they said, Of Haran are we. And he said unto them, Know ye 5 Laban the son of Nahor? And they said, We know him. And he said unto them, Is it well with him? And they 6 said, It is well: and, behold, Rachel his daughter cometh with the sheep. And he said, Lo, it is yet high day, neither 7 is it time that the cattle should be gathered together: water ye the sheep, and go and feed them. And they said, We 8 cannot, until all the flocks be gathered together, and they roll the stone from the well's mouth; then we water the sheep. While he yet spake with them, Rachel came with 9 her father's sheep; for she kept them. And it came to pass, 10 when Jacob saw Rachel the daughter of Laban his mother's brother, and the sheep of Laban his mother's brother, that Jacob went near, and rolled the stone from the well's mouth, and watered the flock of Laban his mother's brother. And 11 Jacob kissed Rachel, and lifted up his voice, and wept. And Jacob told Rachel that he was her father's brother, 12 and that he was Rebekah's son: and she ran and told her father. And it came to pass, when Laban heard the tidings 13 of Jacob his sister's son, that he ran to meet him, and embraced him, and kissed him, and brought him to his house. And he told Laban all these things. And Laban 14

---

4. unto them: i.e. the shepherds of the three flocks.

6. Rachel his daughter. The name means 'ewe,' and is a fitting one for the child of a flock-master.

7. the cattle: a wider word covering all sorts of live stock. Cf. xlvii 16, 17.

should be gathered together: i.e. to be put into the fold for the night.

10. rolled the stone. It was evidently the act of a strong man to displace the heavy stone on the top of the well.

13. kissed him. It was characteristic of Laban to give a rather effusive welcome, cf. xxiv. 31.

said to him, Surely thou art my bone and my flesh. And
he abode with him the space of a month.

15-30. *Jacob's double marriage.*

15 And Laban said unto Jacob, Because thou art my
brother, shouldest thou therefore serve me for nought?
16 tell me, what shall thy wages be? And Laban had two
daughters : the name of the elder was Leah, and the name
17 of the younger was Rachel. And Leah's eyes were tender ;
18 but Rachel was beautiful and well favoured. And Jacob
loved Rachel; and he said, I will serve thee seven years
19 for Rachel thy younger daughter. And Laban said, It is
better that I give her to thee, than that I should give her
20 to another man : abide with me. And Jacob served seven
years for Rachel; and they seemed unto him but a few
21 days, for the love he had to her. And Jacob said unto
Laban, Give me my wife, for my days are fulfilled, that I
22 may go in unto her. And Laban gathered together all
23 the men of the place, and made a feast. And it came to
pass in the evening, that he took Leah his daughter, and
24 brought her to him ; and he went in unto her. And Laban
gave Zilpah his handmaid unto his daughter Leah for an
25 handmaid. And it came to pass in the morning that, behold, it was Leah : and he said to Laban, What is this thou

---

14. my bone and my flesh : cf. ii. 23.

15. brother = kinsman, cf. xiv. 14, xxiv. 48.

16. Leah : the name denotes a species of gazelle.

17. tender : probably = weak, though an ancient writer suggests
that the words imply that Leah's eyes were her best feature.

18. serve thee seven years. It was customary to give sub-
stantial gifts to the bride's father, but Jacob has only his personal
service to offer.

22. made a feast. The marriage feast was a principal feature
in a wedding, cf. Judg. xiv. 10, Matt. xxii. 2, John ii. 1.

23. brought her to him : the bride was always brought in
veiled. Leah seems to have been a ready accomplice.

25. behold, it was Leah. Laban's unscrupulous act was char

hast done unto me? did not I serve with thee for Rachel?
wherefore then hast thou beguiled me? And Laban said, It **26**
is not so done in our place, to give the younger before the
firstborn. Fulfil the week of this one, and we will give thee **27**
the other also for the service which thou shalt serve with
me yet seven other years. And Jacob did so, and fulfilled **28**
her week: and he gave him Rachel his daughter to wife.
And Laban gave to Rachel his daughter Bilhah his hand- **29**
maid to be her handmaid. And he went in also unto Rachel, **30**
and he loved also Rachel more than Leah, and served
with him yet seven other years.

xxix. 31–xxx. 24. *The birth of Jacob's children.*

And the LORD saw that Leah was hated, and he opened **31**
her womb: but Rachel was barren. And Leah conceived, **32**
and bare a son, and she called his name Reuben: for she
said, Because the LORD hath looked upon my affliction;
for now my husband will love me. And she conceived **33**
again, and bare a son; and said, Because the LORD hath
heard that I am hated, he hath therefore given me this

---

acteristic of him, and Jacob the deceiver now knew what it was
to be deceived.

27. Fulfil the week: the marriage festivities lasted a week as
in the case of Samson (Judg. xiv. 12).

we will give thee the other also. In the Levitical law (Lev.
xviii. 18) marriage with two sisters at once is forbidden. But
evidently it was not contrary to custom in primitive times.
Laban thus secures a husband for both his daughters, and at the
same time obtains Jacob's service for 14 years.

xxix. 31–xxx. 24. All Jacob's children, with the exception of
Benjamin, are born in Haran.

31. Leah was hated: the verb is used more or less technically
= 'less loved,' cf. Deut. xxi. 15.

32. Reuben. The derivation 'look on my affliction' rests as
often on a slight similarity of sound, cf. v. 29. The name means
rather 'see! a son.' Some have thought that it may be connected
with one of the numerous Arabic words for 'lion.'

34 *son* also: and she called his name Simeon. And she conceived again, and bare a son; and said, Now this time will
my husband be joined unto me, because I have borne him
35 three sons: therefore was his name called Levi. And she
conceived again, and bare a son: and she said, This time
will I praise the LORD: therefore she called his name
Judah; and she left bearing.

30   And when Rachel saw that she bare Jacob no children,
Rachel envied her sister; and she said unto Jacob, Give
2 me children, or else I die. And Jacob's anger was kindled
against Rachel: and he said, Am I in God's stead, who
3 hath withheld from thee the fruit of the womb? And she
said, Behold my maid Bilhah, go in unto her; that she
may bear upon my knees, and I also may obtain children
4 by her. And she gave him Bilhah her handmaid to wife:
5 and Jacob went in unto her. And Bilhah conceived, and
6 bare Jacob a son. And Rachel said, God hath judged me,
and hath also heard my voice, and hath given me a son:
7 therefore called she his name Dan. And Bilhah Rachel's
handmaid conceived again, and bare Jacob a second son.

---

33. Simeon. The root may well be that of the verb 'to hear,'
cf. I*sh*mael. But it may also be another animal name, 'hyaena.'

34. Levi. The derivation is probable, though some scholars
prefer to regard Levi as = 'belonging to Leah.'

35. Judah. Here the derivation is again probable. It is of
course from Judah that we get the word Jew.

xxx. 2. Am I in God's stead...? God alone is the giver of
children, 1 Sam. i. 27; Ps. cxxvii. 3. For the expression, cf. Gen.
l. 19.

3. she may bear upon my knees. The phrase is usually
applied to the father acknowledging the new born child as his
own, cf. l. 23; Job iii. 12. Here Rachel means that she will
adopt as her own the children of Bilhah.

obtain children: lit. 'be built up,' see note on xvi. 2.

6. God hath judged me. The derivation is without difficulty
and the sense is 'God hath vindicated me,' i.e. 'approved my
action.' For Dan = 'judge' cf. xlix. 16.

And Rachel said, With mighty wrestlings have I wrestled 8
with my sister, and have prevailed: and she called his
name Naphtali. When Leah saw that she had left bearing, 9
she took Zilpah her handmaid, and gave her to Jacob
to wife. And Zilpah Leah's handmaid bare Jacob a son. 10
And Leah said, Fortunate! and she called his name Gad. 11
And Zilpah Leah's handmaid bare Jacob a second son. 12
And Leah said, Happy am I! for the daughters will call me 13
happy: and she called his name Asher. And Reuben went 14
in the days of wheat harvest, and found mandrakes in the
field, and brought them unto his mother Leah. Then
Rachel said to Leah, Give me, I pray thee, of thy son's
mandrakes. And she said unto her, Is it a small matter 15
that thou hast taken away my husband? and wouldest thou
take away my son's mandrakes also? And Rachel said,
Therefore he shall lie with thee to-night for thy son's mandrakes. And Jacob came from the field in the evening, and 16
Leah went out to meet him, and said, Thou must come
in unto me; for I have surely hired thee with my son's

---

8. With mighty wrestlings: lit. 'wrestlings of God.' If the
rendering is correct the expression is a form of superlative, cf.
xxiii. 6, and in the N.T. Acts vii. 20; 2 Cor. x. 4. But it may
mean 'wrestlings (in prayer) with God' and then we might compare the story of Peniel (xxxii. 24).

Naphtali: the root means 'twisted,' 'contorted.'

11. Fortunate! or, according to another reading, 'Fortune
has come.' Gad was a Syrian god of fortune whose name survives
in Baal-gad (Josh. xi. 17) and Migdal-gad (Josh. xv. 37). Cf.
also Isa. lxv. 11.

13. Happy am I! lit. 'in my happiness.' Asher may be connected with this root, or possibly with Asherah, a Canaanite
goddess.

will call me happy: cf. Song of Songs vi. 9; Lk. i. 48.

14. mandrakes: a plant of the Solanum family, bearing a
fruit like a tomato, which ripens in late spring, and from its
heavy, musk-like smell (Song vii. 13) is supposed to act as a
love charm. Mandrake comes from the Latin *mandragora*: R.V.
marg. 'love-apples' is a rendering of the Hebrew word.

17 mandrakes. And he lay with her that night. And God
hearkened unto Leah, and she conceived, and bare Jacob
18 a fifth son. And Leah said, God hath given me my hire,
because I gave my handmaid to my husband: and she
19 called his name Issachar. And Leah conceived again, and
20 bare a sixth son to Jacob. And Leah said, God hath en-
dowed me with a good dowry; now will my husband dwell
with me, because I have borne him six sons: and she called
21 his name Zebulun. And afterwards she bare a daughter,
22 and called her name Dinah. And God remembered Rachel,
23 and God hearkened to her, and opened her womb. And
she conceived, and bare a son: and said, God hath taken
24 away my reproach: and she called his name Joseph, saying, The LORD add to me another son.

xxx. 25–43. *Jacob by his cunning becomes wealthy.*

25   And it came to pass, when Rachel had borne Joseph,
that Jacob said unto Laban, Send me away, that I may
26 go unto mine own place, and to my country. Give me my
wives and my children for whom I have served thee, and
let me go: for thou knowest my service wherewith I have
27 served thee. And Laban said unto him, If now I have
found favour in thine eyes, *tarry: for* I have divined that

---

18. my hire: Issachar is thus connected with the Hebrew
word *sachar* = hire.

20. Two alternative derivations are given for Zebulun: either
from *zabad* = 'endow' or from *zabal* = 'dwell.'

21. Dinah. No etymology is given for the daughter's name,
but it means 'judgment' and is of the same root as Dan.

23. As with Zebulun two derivatives are given for Joseph:
either from *asaph* = 'take away' or *yasaph* = 'add.'

25–43. Laban is represented as selfish and grasping, but in
wits he is no match for Jacob.

25. Send me away. We should rather say 'let me go away.'

27. *tarry.* The word is not in the Hebrew, which breaks off
without an apodosis.

I have divined. The word is a technical one, implying the

the LORD hath blessed me for thy sake. And he said, 28
Appoint me thy wages, and I will give it. And he said 29
unto him, Thou knowest how I have served thee, and how
thy cattle hath fared with me. For it was little which thou 30
hadst before I came, and it hath increased unto a multitude; and the LORD hath blessed thee whithersoever I
turned: and now when shall I provide for mine own house
also? And he said, What shall I give thee? And Jacob 31
said, Thou shalt not give me aught: if thou wilt do this
thing for me, I will again feed thy flock and keep it. I will 32
pass through all thy flock to-day, removing from thence
every speckled and spotted one, and every black one
among the sheep, and the spotted and speckled among
the goats: and *of such* shall be my hire. So shall my 33
righteousness answer for me hereafter, when thou shalt
come concerning my hire that is before thee: every one
that is not speckled and spotted among the goats, and
black among the sheep, that *if found* with me shall be
counted stolen. And Laban said, Behold, I would it might 34
be according to thy word. And he removed that day the 35
he-goats that were ringstraked and spotted, and all the
she-goats that were speckled and spotted, every one that
had white in it, and all the black ones among the sheep,
and gave them into the hand of his sons; and he set three 36
days' journey betwixt himself and Jacob: and Jacob fed
the rest of Laban's flocks. And Jacob took him rods of 37
fresh poplar, and of the almond and of the plane tree;

---

taking of omens. In xliv. 5–15 it refers to hydromancy or divination by water. In Laban's case it may have some connection
with the *teraphim* (xxxi. 19).

32. Jacob proposes to take for himself only the sheep and
goats of unusual colour, leaving the normal animals to Laban.
It is due to his cunning that the unusual animals outnumber the
normal ones.

35. ringstraked: i.e. streaked with rings. So 'strakes' in *v.*
37 = streaks.

and peeled white strakes in them, and made the white
38 appear which was in the rods. And he set the rods which
he had peeled over against the flocks in the gutters in the
watering troughs where the flocks came to drink; and
39 they conceived when they came to drink. And the flocks
conceived before the rods, and the flocks brought forth
40 ringstraked, speckled, and spotted. And Jacob separated
the lambs, and set the faces of the flocks toward the ringstraked and all the black in the flock of Laban; and he
put his own droves apart, and put them not unto Laban's
41 flock. And it came to pass, whensoever the stronger of
the flock did conceive, that Jacob laid the rods before the
eyes of the flock in the gutters, that they might conceive
42 among the rods; but when the flock were feeble, he put
them not in: so the feebler were Laban's, and the stronger
43 Jacob's. And the man increased exceedingly, and had large
flocks, and maidservants and menservants, and camels and
asses.

xxxi. 1–55—xxxii. 2. *Jacob returns from Haran.*

31 And he heard the words of Laban's sons, saying, Jacob
hath taken away all that was our father's; and of that
2 which was our father's hath he gotten all this glory. And
Jacob beheld the countenance of Laban, and, behold, it
3 was not toward him as beforetime. And the LORD said
unto Jacob, Return unto the land of thy fathers, and to

---

38. The ewes looking at the striped rods brought forth striped
lambs. The device is said to be known among shepherds still,
but it was evidently unknown to Laban.

41. Jacob shews his astuteness still further by arranging that
some of the lambs should be white and fall to Laban's share, but
that these should be the offspring of the feebler ewes.

xxxi. 1. all this glory: in the particular sense of wealth, cf.
Ps. xlix. 17.

3. the LORD said: contrast *v.* 11 'the angel of God said.'
The change is typical of the source known as E. in which God's
messages are sent either by angels or by dreams or visions.

thy kindred; and I will be with thee. And Jacob sent 4
and called Rachel and Leah to the field unto his flock, and 5
said unto them, I see your father's countenance, that it is
not toward me as beforetime; but the God of my father
hath been with me. And ye know that with all my power 6
I have served your father. And your father hath deceived 7
me, and changed my wages ten times; but God suffered
him not to hurt me. If he said thus, The speckled shall 8
be thy wages; then all the flock bare speckled: and if he
said thus, The ringstraked shall be thy wages; then bare
all the flock ringstraked. Thus God hath taken away the 9
cattle of your father, and given them to me. And it came 10
to pass at the time that the flock conceived, that I lifted
up mine eyes, and saw in a dream, and, behold, the he-
goats which leaped upon the flock were ringstraked,
speckled, and grisled. And the angel of God said unto 11
me in the dream, Jacob: and I said, Here am I. And he 12
said, Lift up now thine eyes, and see, all the he-goats which
leap upon the flock are ringstraked, speckled, and grisled:
for I have seen all that Laban doeth unto thee. I am the 13
God of Beth-el, where thou anointedst a pillar, where
thou vowedst a vow unto me: now arise, get thee out
from this land, and return unto the land of thy nativity.
And Rachel and Leah answered and said unto him, Is 14
there yet any portion or inheritance for us in our father's
house? Are we not counted of him strangers? for he hath 15

I **will be with thee**: cf. xxvii. 15.

7. changed my wages ten times. This appears to belong to
a different account from that in the last chapter. Here the success
of Jacob in obtaining the bulk of the 'cattle' is represented as
due not to his own cleverness, but to God's help in consequence
of Laban's trickery.

13. the God of Beth-el: is the God who appeared at Beth-el.
But the phrase is an unusual one: lit. 'the God [at] Beth-el.' A
similar construction in 2 Kings xxiii. 17.

15. hath sold us. A bridegroom was expected to pay money

16 sold us, and hath also quite devoured our money. For all
the riches which God hath taken away from our father,
that is ours and our children's: now then, whatsoever God
17 hath said unto thee, do. Then Jacob rose up, and set his
18 sons and his wives upon the camels; and he carried away
all his cattle, and all his substance which he had gathered,
the cattle of his getting, which he had gathered in Paddan-
aram, for to go to Isaac his father unto the land of Canaan.
19 Now Laban was gone to shear his sheep: and Rachel
20 stole the teraphim that were her father's. And Jacob stole
away unawares to Laban the Syrian, in that he told him
21 not that he fled. So he fled with all that he had; and he
rose up, and passed over the River, and set his face toward
the mountain of Gilead.

22 And it was told Laban on the third day that Jacob was
23 fled. And he took his brethren with him, and pursued
after him seven days' journey; and he overtook him in

---

to the bride's father but he usually received presents in exchange.
It was typical of Laban's stinginess that he exacted the fourteen
years' labour from Jacob, but gave nothing to him or his wives.

18. in Paddan-aram. This name for Mesopotamia is an indication that the verse comes from P. Cf. xxv. 20.

19. to shear his sheep. Sheep shearing was a shepherds' fes-
tival which lasted several days, cf. 1 Sam. xxv. 2; 2 Sam. xiii.
23.

the teraphim. Apparently household gods, like the Latin
Penates. From 1 Sam. xix. 13-16 it is obvious that they were,
sometimes at any rate, of human size and shape. Though the
word is plural it may possibly refer to a single image. Teraphim
were a relic of superstition which survived a long time, cf. 2 Kings
xxiii. 24; Ezek. xxi. 21; Hos. iii. 4; Zech. x. 2.

21. the River. Here, as usually when standing by itself, = the
Euphrates. In such cases R.V. prints with capital, cf. Josh.
xxiv. 2; 1 Kings iv. 21, 24, etc.

23. his brethren: i.e. his kinsfolk.

seven days' journey. The distance from Haran to Gilead is
about 350 miles. Allowing Jacob three days' start it would still
be difficult for flocks and herds to cover the distance in 10 days.
It has been suggested that E., to which this narrative is assigned
(cf. v. 24), placed Laban's home somewhere in the eastern desert.

the mountain of Gilead. And God came to Laban the 24
Syrian in a dream of the night, and said unto him, Take
heed to thyself that thou speak not to Jacob either good
or bad. And Laban came up with Jacob. Now Jacob 25
had pitched his tent in the mountain: and Laban with his
brethren pitched in the mountain of Gilead. And Laban 26
said to Jacob, What hast thou done, that thou hast stolen
away unawares to me, and carried away my daughters as
captives of the sword? Wherefore didst thou flee secretly, 27
and steal away from me; and didst not tell me, that I
might have sent thee away with mirth and with songs,
with tabret and with harp; and hast not suffered me to 28
kiss my sons and my daughters? now hast thou done
foolishly. It is in the power of my hand to do you hurt: 29
but the God of your father spake unto me yesternight,
saying, Take heed to thyself that thou speak not to Jacob
either good or bad. And now, *though* thou wouldest needs 30
be gone, because thou sore longedst after thy father's house,
yet wherefore hast thou stolen my gods? And Jacob 31
answered and said to Laban, Because I was afraid: for
I said, Lest thou shouldest take thy daughters from me
by force. With whomsoever thou findest thy gods, he 32
shall not live: before our brethren discern thou what is

---

25. in the mountain. The name seems omitted: possibly it
was Mizpah (*v.* 49).

26. as captives of the sword. Laban represents that Jacob
has carried off Leah and Rachel by violence during their father's
temporary absence from home.

27. tabret: a kind of tambourine or drum. The same Hebrew
word is sometimes translated 'timbrel.' Cf. Exod. xv. 20.

28. kiss: i.e. in farewell, cf. Ruth i. 14.

29. in the power of my hand: a phrase occurring several times,
Deut. xxviii. 32; Mic. ii. 1; Prov. iii. 27.

30. my gods: i.e. the teraphim, cf. xxxv. 2.

32. Jacob indignantly repudiates the charge of having stolen
the teraphim, as his sons later repudiate the charge of having
stolen Joseph's cup, cf. xliv. 7-9.

thine with me, and take it to thee. For Jacob knew not
33 that Rachel had stolen them. And Laban went into Jacob's
tent, and into Leah's tent, and into the tent of the two
maidservants; but he found them not. And he went out
34 of Leah's tent, and entered into Rachel's tent. Now Rachel
had taken the teraphim, and put them in the camel's furniture, and sat upon them. And Laban felt about all the
35 tent, and found them not. And she said to her father, Let
not my lord be angry that I cannot rise up before thee;
for the manner of women is upon me. And he searched,
36 but found not the teraphim. And Jacob was wroth, and
chode with Laban: and Jacob answered and said to Laban,
What is my trespass? what is my sin, that thou hast hotly
37 pursued after me? Whereas thou hast felt about all my
stuff, what hast thou found of all thy household stuff? Set
it here before my brethren and thy brethren, that they may
38 judge betwixt us two. This twenty years have I been with
thee; thy ewes and thy she-goats have not cast their
39 young, and the rams of thy flocks have I not eaten. That
which was torn of beasts I brought not unto thee; I bare
the loss of it; of my hand didst thou require it, whether
40 stolen by day or stolen by night. Thus I was; in the day
the drought consumed me, and the frost by night; and
41 my sleep fled from mine eyes. These twenty years have
I been in thy house; I served thee fourteen years for thy
two daughters, and six years for thy flock: and thou hast
42 changed my wages ten times. Except the God of my

---

34. the camel's furniture: probably the wicker framework of
the camel's saddle or palanquin. It is characteristic of the humour
which occasionally gleams through these early narratives that
while Laban is searching unsuccessfully for the teraphim, Rachel
is all the time sitting on them.

36. Jacob bursts out into an indignant denunciation of Laban's
whole treatment of him.

38. the rams...have I not eaten. Contrast the conduct of the
wicked shepherds in Ezek. xxxiv. 3.

41. ten times: cf. *v.* 7.

father, the God of Abraham, and the Fear of Isaac, had been with me, surely now hadst thou sent me away empty. God hath seen mine affliction and the labour of my hands, and rebuked thee yesternight. And Laban answered and 43 said unto Jacob, The daughters are my daughters, and the children are my children, and the flocks are my flocks, and all that thou seest is mine: and what can I do this day unto these my daughters, or unto their children which they have borne? And now come, let us make a cove- 44 nant, I and thou; and let it be for a witness between me and thee. And Jacob took a stone, and set it up for a 45 pillar. And Jacob said unto his brethren, Gather stones; 46 and they took stones, and made an heap: and they did eat there by the heap. And Laban called it Jegar-saha- 47 dutha: but Jacob called it Galeed. And Laban said, This 48 heap is witness between me and thee this day. Therefore was the name of it called Galeed: and Mizpah, for he said, 49 The LORD watch between me and thee, when we are absent one from another. If thou shalt afflict my daugh- 50

---

42. the Fear of Isaac: i.e. the God whom Isaac feared. The title is apparently an old one.

rebuked thee: cf. *v.* 24.

44. let it be for a witness. Unless the covenant was written it is difficult to see how it could be a witness. Possibly we should read 'and God shall be for a witness,' cf. *v.* 52.

45. Jacob took a stone. There seems to be some confusion. More probably Laban took the stone which formed a *maṣṣēbah* or pillar, and Jacob made the heap of stones.

46. they did eat. A covenant was ratified by means of a solemn meal, *v.* 54. Cf. Exod. xxiv. 11.

47. The two words are respectively Aramaic and Hebrew for 'the heap of witness.' But Galeed is not really Gilead, which means rather 'stony' or 'rocky.' So the derivation is not strictly correct. Possibly a striking boundary stone marked the limits of the Hebrew and Aramaic speaking peoples.

49. and Mizpah. Apparently two traditions are combined, for the same place would not be called Galeed and Mizpah. The latter word means 'watch tower,' a common name for a hill.

ters, and if thou shalt take wives beside my daughters, no
man is with us: see, God is witness betwixt me and thee.
51 And Laban said to Jacob, Behold this heap, and behold
52 the pillar, which I have set betwixt me and thee. This
heap be witness, and the pillar be witness, that I will not
pass over this heap to thee, and that thou shalt not pass
53 over this heap and this pillar unto me, for harm. The
God of Abraham, and the God of Nahor, the God of their
father, judge betwixt us. And Jacob sware by the Fear
54 of his father Isaac. And Jacob offered a sacrifice in the
mountain, and called his brethren to eat bread: and they
55 did eat bread, and tarried all night in the mountain. And
early in the morning Laban rose up, and kissed his sons
and his daughters, and blessed them: and Laban de-
32 parted, and returned unto his place. And Jacob went on
2 his way, and the angels of God met him. And Jacob said
when he saw them, This is God's host: and he called the
name of that place Mahanaim.

xxxii. 3–21. *Jacob prepares to meet Esau.*

3   And Jacob sent messengers before him to Esau his
4 brother unto the land of Seir, the field of Edom. And he

---

50. take wives beside my daughters. A similar stipulation
is found in Babylonian marriage contracts.

53. The God of Abraham, and the God of Nahor. Abraham
and Nahor represent the ancestors of the Hebrews and Aramaeans
respectively, and apparently the God of each is regarded as distinct, for the verb 'judge' is in the plural.

xxxii. 1. the angels of God. It may be that the angels are
conceived of as welcoming Jacob back to the land which was
regarded as the special possession of the God Who had appeared
to him.

2. Mahanaim: strictly = 'the double camp' or 'host.' The
place was important in later times. Cf. 2 Sam. ii. 8, xvii. 24;
1 Kings ii. 8.

3. the field of Edom. Esau's migration to this part of the
land is not actually mentioned till xxxvi. 6–8.

commanded them, saying, Thus shall ye say unto my lord
Esau; Thus saith thy servant Jacob, I have sojourned
with Laban, and stayed until now: and I have oxen, and 5
asses *and* flocks, and menservants and maidservants: and
I have sent to tell my lord, that I may find grace in thy
sight. And the messengers returned to Jacob, saying, We 6
came to thy brother Esau, and moreover he cometh to
meet thee, and four hundred men with him. Then Jacob 7
was greatly afraid and was distressed: and he divided the
people that was with him, and the flocks, and the herds, and
the camels, into two companies; and he said, If Esau come 8
to the one company, and smite it, then the company which
is left shall escape. And Jacob said, O God of my father 9
Abraham, and God of my father Isaac, O LORD, which
saidst to me, Return unto thy country, and to thy kindred, and I will do thee good: I am not worthy of the 10
least of all the mercies, and of all the truth, which thou
hast shewed unto thy servant; for with my staff I passed
over this Jordan; and now I am become two companies.
Deliver me, I pray thee, from the hand of my brother, 11
from the hand of Esau: for I fear him, lest he come and
smite me, the mother with the children. And thou saidst, 12
I will surely do thee good, and make thy seed as the sand

---

4. thy servant Jacob. Jacob's message is very humble: contrast xxvii. 29. But it is also diplomatic for it wins over Esau,
who with his large force seems to have approached with hostile
intent.

7. into two companies: or 'camps.' Apparently we have here
another explanation of the name Mahanaim.

9. Jacob's fine prayer is constructed after the same kind of
fashion as a Collect. It begins with an invocation recalling God's
mercies, followed by a confession and a prayer, and ending with
the claiming of the fulfilment of God's promise.

10. truth: i.e. faithfulness to promise. For the combination
mercy and truth cf. 2 Sam. ii. 6 (Hebr.); Ps. xl. 11, etc.

11. the mother with the children: lit. 'upon the children,' i.e.
standing over them. A proverbial expression, cf. Hos. x. 14.

13 of the sea, which cannot be numbered for multitude. And
   he lodged there that night; and took of that which he had
14 with him a present for Esau his brother; two hundred she-
   goats and twenty he-goats, two hundred ewes and twenty
15 rams, thirty milch camels and their colts, forty kine and
16 ten bulls, twenty she-asses and ten foals. And he delivered
   them into the hand of his servants, every drove by itself;
   and said unto his servants, Pass over before me, and put
17 a space betwixt drove and drove. And he commanded
   the foremost, saying, When Esau my brother meeteth
   thee, and asketh thee, saying, Whose art thou? and whither
18 goest thou? and whose are these before thee? then thou
   shalt say, *They be* thy servant Jacob's; it is a present sent
   unto my lord Esau: and, behold, he also is behind us.
19 And he commanded also the second, and the third, and
   all that followed the droves, saying, On this manner shall
20 ye speak unto Esau, when ye find him; and ye shall say,
   Moreover, behold, thy servant Jacob is behind us. For
   he said, I will appease him with the present that goeth
   before me, and afterward I will see his face; peradventure
21 he will accept me. So the present passed over before him:
   and he himself lodged that night in the company.

22–32. *Jacob at Peniel.*

22 And he rose up that night, and took his two wives, and
   his two handmaids, and his eleven children, and passed

---

13. a present: a technical word denoting a present to secure
the goodwill of a superior. Cf. xliii. 11.

16. Jacob hopes by the continuous arrival of fresh and more
valuable presents to appease his brother's wrath. Compare Abigail's present to David, 1 Sam. xxv. 18. At the same time his
heart is filled with anxious fears.

20. thy servant Jacob is behind us. So Abigail followed up
her present to David (1 Sam. xxv. 18, 19).

appease him: lit. 'cover his face'; so 'propitiate.' The verb
later assumed the technical sense of 'make propitiation.'

22. passed over the ford of Jabbok. Yet in the next verse he

over the ford of Jabbok. And he took them, and sent 23
them over the stream, and sent over that he had. And 24
Jacob was left alone; and there wrestled a man with him
until the breaking of the day. And when he saw that he 25
prevailed not against him, he touched the hollow of his
thigh; and the hollow of Jacob's thigh was strained, as
he wrestled with him. And he said, Let me go, for the 26
day breaketh. And he said, I will not let thee go, except
thou bless me. And he said unto him, What is thy name? 27
And he said, Jacob. And he said, Thy name shall be 28
called no more Jacob, but Israel: for thou hast striven
with God and with men, and hast prevailed. And Jacob 29
asked him, and said, Tell me, I pray thee, thy name. And
he said, Wherefore is it that thou dost ask after my name?

---

is represented as not passing over himself. The Jabbok is a
large tributary of the Jordan on its left bank: modern Zerka or
Blue River.

24. was left alone. Apparently he had formed the habit of
retiring for solitary prayer.

there wrestled a man. The story is evidently a picture rather
than literal history, and the wrestling is wrestling in prayer.
Jacob starts with the object of praying for help in a special
trouble: but he is led on to a deeper spiritual experience as a
result of which he seems to win his way into the very presence
of God, and obtains a blessing of which his changed name is the
token. At the same time his spiritual struggle leaves a physical
result in the strained sinew. Compare the reference to this struggle
in Hos. xii. 4.

26. for the day breaketh. The spiritual lesson of the story is
bound up with traces of superstition: so the antagonist is regarded as a spirit of the night who must disappear before dawn.

27. What is thy name? The blessing is to be closely associated
with the change of name.

28. Israel. The word should strictly mean 'God striveth.'
But it might possibly mean 'one who strives with God.' Cf.
Jerubbaal = one who strives with Baal (Judg. vi. 32) though here
too the more probable meaning is 'Baal strives' or 'may Baal
strive.'

29. Tell me...thy name. Jacob asks the same question as his
antagonist. 'The name' in Hebrew thought covers almost the
whole personality. For the refusal to tell the name cf. Judg. xiii. 18.

30 And he blessed him there. And Jacob called the name
   of the place Peniel: for, *said he*, I have seen God face to
31 face, and my life is preserved. And the sun rose upon him
   as he passed over Penuel, and he halted upon his thigh.
32 Therefore the children of Israel eat not the sinew of the
   hip which is upon the hollow of the thigh, unto this day:
   because he touched the hollow of Jacob's thigh in the
   sinew of the hip.

xxxiii. *The meeting between Jacob and Esau: Jacob goes to Shechem.*

33   And Jacob lifted up his eyes, and looked, and, behold,
       Esau came, and with him four hundred men. And he
       divided the children unto Leah, and unto Rachel, and unto
2 the two handmaids. And he put the handmaids and their
   children foremost, and Leah and her children after, and
3 Rachel and Joseph hindermost. And he himself passed
   over before them, and bowed himself to the ground seven
4 times, until he came near to his brother. And Esau ran
   to meet him, and embraced him, and fell on his neck, and
5 kissed him: and they wept. And he lifted up his eyes,
   and saw the women and the children; and said, Who are
   these with thee? And he said, The children which God

---

30. Peniel: means God's face. Penuel is merely a variant, the
former being strictly a genitive and the latter a nominative form.

32. eat not the sinew. It is curious that this is nowhere else
mentioned in the O.T., though obviously it was a recognized
custom at the time when this account was written.

xxxiii. 3. bowed himself...seven times. A mark of deepest
reverence. This phrase occurs repeatedly in the Tel-el-Amarna
tablets 'At the foot of the king seven times and seven times do
I fall.'

4. ran to meet him. His welcome was as spontaneous and
warm as that which the father gave to the Prodigal Son in St Luke
xv. 20. Jewish tradition has found it hard to believe in such
magnanimity.

they wept. So Joseph wept for joy at meeting his brothers
again, Gen. xlv. 14, 15.

hath graciously given thy servant. Then the handmaids 6
came near, they and their children, and they bowed themselves. And Leah also and her children came near, and 7
bowed themselves: and after came Joseph near and
Rachel, and they bowed themselves. And he said, What 8
meanest thou by all this company which I met? And he
said, To find grace in the sight of my lord. And Esau 9
said, I have enough; my brother, let that thou hast be
thine. And Jacob said, Nay, I pray thee, if now I have 10
found grace in thy sight, then receive my present at my
hand: forasmuch as I have seen thy face, as one seeth
the face of God, and thou wast pleased with me. Take, 11
I pray thee, my gift that is brought to thee; because God
hath dealt graciously with me, and because I have enough.
And he urged him, and he took it. And he said, Let us 12
take our journey, and let us go, and I will go before thee.
And he said unto him, My lord knoweth that the children 13
are tender, and that the flocks and herds with me give
suck: and if they overdrive them one day, all the flocks
will die. Let my lord, I pray thee, pass over before his 14
servant: and I will lead on softly, according to the pace
of the cattle that is before me and according to the pace
of the children, until I come unto my lord unto Seir. And 15
Esau said, Let me now leave with thee some of the folk
that are with me. And he said, What needeth it? let me
find grace in the sight of my lord. So Esau returned 16

---

8. this company: lit. 'camp.' Esau refers thus to the lordly
present which Jacob had sent on before him.

10. as one seeth the face of God. A somewhat elaborate com-
pliment which seems to contain an allusion to the name Peniel.
Or perhaps Jacob recognizes heaven-sent kindliness in Esau's face.

12. I will go before thee: i.e. as a protection. Jacob, however,
perhaps with the memory of Laban in his mind, is afraid lest his
brother should become less amiable.

14. unto Seir. Jacob professes an intention to visit his brother
in his home, but he takes no steps to carry it out.

17 that day on his way unto Seir. And Jacob journeyed
   to Succoth, and built him an house, and made booths
   for his cattle: therefore the name of the place is called
   Succoth.

18   And Jacob came in peace to the city of Shechem, which
   is in the land of Canaan, when he came from Paddan-
19 aram; and encamped before the city. And he bought the
   parcel of ground, where he had spread his tent, at the
   hand of the children of Hamor, Shechem's father, for an
20 hundred pieces of money. And he erected there an altar,
   and called it El-elohe-Israel.

xxxiv. *The outrage on Dinah and its sequel.*

34   And Dinah the daughter of Leah, which she bare unto
 2 Jacob, went out to see the daughters of the land. And

---

17. made booths. Succoth means 'booths.' The site is
uncertain. It is mentioned in Josh. xiii. 27; Judg. viii. 5 ff.;
Ps. lx. 6.

18. in peace. The R.V. marg. 'to Shalem, a city of Shechem'
is possible, and is supported by some of the Versions, and by the
fact that there was a place of that name not far from Shechem.
But the text is probably right. Shechem was Abraham's first
stopping place in the land, cf. xii. 6.

19. pieces of money: the word occurs again only in Josh.
xxiv. 32; Job xlii. 11. It seems to mean 'lamb' and possibly it
represents the worth of a lamb in money. There was no coined
money till a much later date, cf. xxiii. 16.

20. erected...an altar. The verb is nowhere else used of building
an altar. Hence there is a good deal to be said for the suggestion
to read 'standing stone' (*maṣṣēbah*) for 'altar,' cf. xxviii. 18.

called it El-elohe-Israel. It has been suggested that the altar
(or pillar) represented God to Jacob. But it may be a contrac-
tion for 'the altar of El-elohe-Israel,' in the same kind of way
as we speak of St Paul's.

xxxiv. It would seem that Jacob had dwelt several years at
Shechem during which time Dinah, who was his youngest child,
had had time to grow up. The story presents several difficulties,
and there seem to be two threads woven together in it. The
sequel seems to be that the tribes of Levi and Simeon were
reduced to great weakness.

Shechem the son of Hamor the Hivite, the prince of the land, saw her; and he took her, and lay with her, and humbled her. And his soul clave unto Dinah the daughter 3 of Jacob, and he loved the damsel, and spake kindly unto the damsel. And Shechem spake unto his father Hamor, 4 saying, Get me this damsel to wife. Now Jacob heard that 5 he had defiled Dinah his daughter; and his sons were with his cattle in the field: and Jacob held his peace until they came. And Hamor the father of Shechem went out 6 unto Jacob to commune with him. And the sons of Jacob 7 came in from the field when they heard it: and the men were grieved, and they were very wroth, because he had wrought folly in Israel in lying with Jacob's daughter; which thing ought not to be done. And Hamor communed 8 with them, saying, The soul of my son Shechem longeth for your daughter: I pray you give her unto him to wife. And make ye marriages with us; give your daughters 9 unto us, and take our daughters unto you. And ye shall 10 dwell with us: and the land shall be before you; dwell and trade ye therein, and get you possessions therein. And 11 Shechem said unto her father and unto her brethren, Let me find grace in your eyes, and what ye shall say unto me I will give. Ask me never so much dowry and gift, and 12 I will give according as ye shall say unto me: but give me the damsel to wife. And the sons of Jacob answered 13

---

3. spake kindly: lit. 'to (*or* upon) the heart.' Cf. l. 21; Isa. xl. 2, etc.

4. spake unto his father Hamor. It was the parent's business to arrange marriages for their sons. Cf. Judg. xiv. 2.

7. ought not to be done: or, perhaps, 'is not done.' It is noticeable that such a breach of morality is unreservedly condemned.

8. communed with them. The brothers are associated with their father in the discussions as to their sister's marriage. So 'our daughter' in *v.* 17.

12. dowry: the gift given by the bridegroom to the bride's father, not, as our word would suggest, the father's gift to the bride.

Shechem and Hamor his father with guile, and spake,
14 because he had defiled Dinah their sister, and said unto
them, We cannot do this thing, to give our sister to one
that is uncircumcised; for that were a reproach unto us:
15 only on this condition will we consent unto you: if ye will
16 be as we be, that every male of you be circumcised; then
will we give our daughters unto you, and we will take your
daughters to us, and we will dwell with you, and we will
17 become one people. But if ye will not hearken unto us,
to be circumcised; then will we take our daughter, and
18 we will be gone. And their words pleased Hamor, and
19 Shechem Hamor's son. And the young man deferred not
to do the thing, because he had delight in Jacob's daughter: and he was honoured above all the house of his father.
20 And Hamor and Shechem his son came unto the gate of
their city, and communed with the men of their city, say-
21 ing, These men are peaceable with us; therefore let them
dwell in the land, and trade therein; for, behold, the land
is large enough for them; let us take their daughters to
22 us for wives, and let us give them our daughters. Only
on this condition will the men consent unto us to dwell
with us, to become one people, if every male among us
23 be circumcised, as they are circumcised. Shall not their
cattle and their substance and all their beasts be ours?
only let us consent unto them, and they will dwell with us.
24 And unto Hamor and unto Shechem his son hearkened
all that went out of the gate of his city; and every male
was circumcised, all that went out of the gate of his city.

---

13. spake: the verb may possibly mean 'laid a snare for.'

16. will we give our daughters. The brothers propose that
when the condition of circumcision has been fulfilled, general
intermarriage should take place between the two clans.

20. unto the gate of their city: i.e. the broad place just inside the gate where public business was transacted. Cf. xix. 1;
Ruth iv. 1.

24. all that went out...his city: i.e. the whole of the people

And it came to pass on the third day, when they were 25
sore, that two of the sons of Jacob, Simeon and Levi,
Dinah's brethren, took each man his sword, and came
upon the city unawares, and slew all the males. And they 26
slew Hamor and Shechem his son with the edge of the
sword, and took Dinah out of Shechem's house, and went
forth. The sons of Jacob came upon the slain, and spoiled 27
the city, because they had defiled their sister. They took 28
their flocks and their herds and their asses, and that which
was in the city, and that which was in the field ; and all their 29
wealth, and all their little ones and their wives, took they
captive and spoiled, even all that was in the house. And 30
Jacob said to Simeon and Levi, Ye have troubled me, to
make me to stink among the inhabitants of the land, among
the Canaanites and the Perizzites: and, I being few in number, they will gather themselves together against me and
smite me ; and I shall be destroyed, I and my house. And 31
they said, Should he deal with our sister as with an harlot?

xxxv. 1–8. *Jacob at Beth-el.*

And God said unto Jacob, Arise, go up to Beth-el, and **35**

---

of the city, there being apparently but one gate. Cf. xxxii. 10,
18 ('went *in*').

27. The sons of Jacob. Apparently all the sons of Jacob are
associated in the deed of treachery, not, as in the other account,
only Simeon and Levi. It is on account of this deed that Simeon
and Levi are singled out for reprobation in Jacob's blessing,
xlix. 5, 6.

30. have troubled me. The same word is used in the story
of Achan (Josh. vi. 18). Cf. also Judg. xi. 35.

to make me to stink : or, as we say, 'to bring me into bad
odour.' A fairly common metaphor, cf. Exod. v. 21 ; 1 Sam.
xiii. 4. Contrast 2 Cor. ii. 15 ; Eph. v. 2.

the Canaanites and the Perizzites. Mentioned together again
in xiii. 7 ; cf. also Judg. i. 4, 5. 'Canaanite' is a general name
for the ancient inhabitants of the land, and 'Perizzite' may possibly
denote village dwellers.

xxxv. 1. God said. The manner of communication is not

dwell there: and make there an altar unto God, who appeared unto thee when thou fleddest from the face of Esau
2 thy brother. Then Jacob said unto his household, and to all that were with him, Put away the strange gods that are among you, and purify yourselves, and change your gar-
3 ments: and let us arise, and go up to Beth-el; and I will make there an altar unto God, who answered me in the day of my distress, and was with me in the way which I
4 went. And they gave unto Jacob all the strange gods which were in their hand, and the rings which were in their ears; and Jacob hid them under the oak which was by Shechem.
5 And they journeyed: and a great terror was upon the cities that were round about them, and they did not pursue after
6 the sons of Jacob. So Jacob came to Luz, which is in the land of Canaan (the same is Beth-el), he and all the people
7 that were with him. And he built there an altar, and called the place El-beth-el: because there God was revealed
8 unto him, when he fled from the face of his brother. And

---

mentioned, but as the narrative comes from the source known as E, it was probably regarded as being an inward monition, not conveyed by an external appearance.

2. Put away the strange gods: cf. Judg. x. 16; 1 Sam. vii. 3. Haran was regarded as a half-heathen land, and the people who had come with Jacob from there would naturally have brought with them objects of superstition and things connected with idols. So Rachel had stolen the teraphim (xxxi. 19).

purify yourselves: i.e. by washings.

change your garments: cf. xli. 14; 2 Sam. xii. 20.

4. the rings. Such were apparently used as charms, cf. Exod. xxxii. 2.

the oak. Evidently a famous landmark at Shechem, cf. xii. 6; Josh. xxiv. 26.

5. a great terror. This may be a correct rendering of the Heb. 'a terror of God,' cf. xxiii. 6. Or it may be rather 'a terror caused by God.'

7. he built there an altar. Before he had merely erected a pillar, xxviii. 18.

was revealed. The verb is in the plural, so 'God' probably stands for 'the angels of God.'

Deborah Rebekah's nurse died, and she was buried below Beth-el under the oak : and the name of it was called Allon-bacuth.

9-15. *Jacob becomes Israel.*

And God appeared unto Jacob again, when he came 9 from Paddan-aram, and blessed him. And God said unto 10 him, Thy name is Jacob : thy name shall not be called any more Jacob, but Israel shall be thy name : and he called his name Israel. And God said unto him, I am God Al- 11 mighty : be fruitful and multiply ; a nation and a company of nations shall be of thee, and kings shall come out of thy loins ; and the land which I gave unto Abraham and 12 Isaac, to thee I will give it, and to thy seed after thee will I give the land. And God went up from him in the place 13 where he spake with him. And Jacob set up a pillar in the 14 place where he spake with him, a pillar of stone : and he poured out a drink offering thereon, and poured oil there-on. And Jacob called the name of the place where God 15 spake with him, Beth-el.

16-22. *The death of Rachel.*

And they journeyed from Beth-el ; and there was still 16 some way to come to Ephrath : and Rachel travailed, and

---

8. Deborah. This is the only place in which she is named, though she is mentioned in xxiv. 59. The name means 'bee.'

9-15. The section seems to be an alternative account of both xxviii. 10-19 and xxxii. 22-28. The style and language of most of it is characteristic of P. With *v.* 10 cf. xvii. 5 : with *v.* 11, xvii. 1, 5, 6.

10. Israel shall be thy name. With the same kind of words Abram's name was changed, Gen. xvii. 5 ; cf. xxxii. 27.

11. be fruitful and multiply. The terms of the blessing are closely similar to that which was given to Abraham, xvii. 6-8.

14. set up a pillar. A parallel account to xxviii. 18.

a drink offering. The first mention of a term that afterwards became common. Cf. Exod. xxix. 40 f. ; Numb. xv. 5, etc.

16. some way to come. The same expression in xlviii. 7

17 she had hard labour. And it came to pass, when she was
 in hard labour, that the midwife said unto her, Fear not;
18 for now thou shalt have another son. And it came to pass, as
 her soul was in departing (for she died), that she called
 his name Ben-oni: but his father called him Benjamin.
19 And Rachel died, and was buried in the way to Ephrath
20 (the same is Beth-lehem). And Jacob set up a pillar upon
 her grave: the same is the Pillar of Rachel's grave unto
21 this day. And Israel journeyed, and spread his tent be-
22 yond the tower of Eder. And it came to pass, while Israel
 dwelt in that land, that Reuben went and lay with Bilhah
 his father's concubine: and Israel heard of it.

23–29. *Jacob's sons. Death and burial of Isaac.*

23   Now the sons of Jacob were twelve: the sons of Leah;

(referring to this passage) and 2 Kings v. 19. The meaning is
uncertain. The Syrian version renders by 'parasang' = about
10 miles.

17. another son: recalling her prayer at the birth of Joseph
(xxx. 24).

18. her soul was in departing. The soul, or principle of life,
is regarded as leaving the body at the moment of death, cf.
1 Kings xvii. 21, 22.

Ben-oni: means 'Son of my sorrow,' but Jacob avoids such an
ill-omened name by changing it to Benjamin = 'son of the right
hand.'

19. Ephrath (the same is Beth-lehem). The identification of
Ephrath with Beth-lehem is supported by xlviii. 7; Ruth iv. 11
and Micah v. 2. But another tradition places it north of Jerusalem.
So in Jer. xxxi. 15 Rachel is represented as speaking from Ramah,
and in 1 Sam. x. 2 her sepulchre is placed in the border of
Benjamin.

20. a pillar: here a tomb-stone, cf. 2 Sam. xviii. 18. It is
noticeable that wherever a 'pillar' is mentioned in Genesis it is
always connected with Jacob. Cf. xxviii. 18, 22, xxxi. 13, 45,
51, 52, xxxv. 14.

21. the tower of Eder: i.e. 'of the flock.' The situation is
unknown: it is not to be identified with the 'tower of the flock'
in Micah iv. 8 which seems to refer to Jerusalem.

22. Reuben's deed of shame is alluded to in xlix. 4.

Reuben, Jacob's firstborn, and Simeon, and Levi, and
Judah, and Issachar, and Zebulun: the sons of Rachel; 24
Joseph and Benjamin: and the sons of Bilhah, Rachel's 25
handmaid; Dan and Naphtali: and the sons of Zilpah, 26
Leah's handmaid; Gad and Asher: these are the sons of
Jacob, which were born to him in Paddan-aram. And Jacob 27
came unto Isaac his father to Mamre, to Kiriath-arba (the
same is Hebron), where Abraham and Isaac sojourned.
And the days of Isaac were an hundred and fourscore 28
years. And Isaac gave up the ghost, and died, and was 29
gathered unto his people, old and full of days; and Esau
and Jacob his sons buried him.

xxxvi. *The generations of Esau.*

Now these are the generations of Esau (the same is **36**

---

27. unto Isaac. The last notice of Isaac was in xxxi. 18. It
is certainly curious to find him still alive, for in xxvii. 14, 80 years
before, he was represented as an old man on the point of death.

Kiriath-arba: cf. xxiii. 2.

28. For the ages of the other patriarchs cf. xxv. 7, xlvii. 28,
l. 26.

29. Esau and Jacob. The two sons are associated in this
last office to their father. So in xxv. 9 Isaac and Ishmael bury
Abraham.

xxxvi. Just as in xxv. P. noted the descendants of Ishmael
before he went on to the main stream of history as represented
by Isaac, so here he gives details of the descendants of Esau,
before passing on to the fortunes of the children of Jacob. The
chapter, though from the list of names it appears very dull, really
contains a good deal of antiquarian and historical interest. It
illustrates the peculiar fondness of the Jews of later times for
genealogies and the care which they devoted to research into the
history of families.

The only way to study the chapter is to make genealogical
trees. Then it becomes evident that there are four separate lists:

1. The descendants of Esau by his three wives Adah, Basemath and Oholibamah.

2. The ancient Horite clans under their seven 'dukes.'

3. A list of eight kings all of different families, the monarchy
not being hereditary.

2 Edom). Esau took his wives of the daughters of Canaan;
 Adah the daughter of Elon the Hittite, and Oholibamah
 the daughter of Anah, the daughter of Zibeon the Hivite;
3 and Basemath Ishmael's daughter, sister of Nebaioth.
4 And Adah bare to Esau Eliphaz; and Basemath bare Reuel;
5 and Oholibamah bare Jeush, and Jalam, and Korah : these
 are the sons of Esau, which were born unto him in the
6 land of Canaan. And Esau took his wives, and his sons,
 and his daughters, and all the souls of his house, and his
 cattle, and all his beasts, and all his possessions, which he
 had gathered in the land of Canaan; and went into a land
7 away from his brother Jacob. For their substance was too
 great for them to dwell together; and the land of their so-
8 journings could not bear them because of their cattle. And
9 Esau dwelt in mount Seir : Esau is Edom. And these

---

4. A list of eleven 'dukes that came of Esau.'

The lists explain among other things how Esau's descendants
were connected with the ancient Horite inhabitants of Edom. So
Oholibamah Esau's third wife is a daughter of Anah one of the
seven Horite dukes : and Timna the concubine of Eliphaz and
mother of Amalek is sister of Lotan another Horite duke. In
vv. 11, 12 Eliphaz has six sons, whereas in *v.* 15 he has seven,
corresponding to the seven sons of Seir (*vv.* 20, 21). Korah has
apparently come in from *v.* 14.

Many of the names do not appear elsewhere and some of the
forms are curious : the frequency of the termination *-an* is to be
noticed.

2. Esau's wives as given in xxvi. 34, xxviii. 9 are Judith,
daughter of Beeri the Hittite, Basemath, daughter of Elon the
Hittite, and Mahalath, daughter of Ishmael and sister of Nebaioth. There are clearly two different accounts, though both seem
to come from P.

the Hivite. Perhaps a mistake for the 'Horite,' cf. *v.* 24. The
Horites were a primitive Edomite people, and their name means
'cave dweller.' The mountainous country of Edom is particularly
rich in caves. So Obadiah speaks of the Edomites as dwelling
'in the clefts of the rock ' (Obad. 3).

4. **Eliphaz.** Probably an Edomite name. Eliphaz the Tema-
nite the friend of Job (Job ii. 11) was an Edomite.

7. Esau is represented as parting from Jacob for the same
reason as that which led Abram and Lot to separate (xiii. 6).

are the generations of Esau the father of the Edomites in
mount Seir: these are the names of Esau's sons; Eliphaz 10
the son of Adah the wife of Esau, Reuel the son of Basemath the wife of Esau. And the sons of Eliphaz were 11
Teman, Omar, Zepho, and Gatam, and Kenaz. And Timna 12
was concubine to Eliphaz Esau's son; and she bare to
Eliphaz Amalek: these are the sons of Adah Esau's wife.
And these are the sons of Reuel; Nahath, and Zerah, 13
Shammah, and Mizzah: these were the sons of Basemath
Esau's wife. And these were the sons of Oholibamah the 14
daughter of Anah, the daughter of Zibeon, Esau's wife:
and she bare to Esau Jeush, and Jalam, and Korah. These 15
are the dukes of the sons of Esau: the sons of Eliphaz the
firstborn of Esau; duke Teman, duke Omar, duke Zepho,
duke Kenaz, duke Korah, duke Gatam, duke Amalek: 16
these are the dukes that came of Eliphaz in the land of
Edom; these are the sons of Adah. And these are the 17
sons of Reuel Esau's son; duke Nahath, duke Zerah, duke
Shammah, duke Mizzah: these are the dukes that came
of Reuel in the land of Edom; these are the sons of
Basemath Esau's wife. And these are the sons of Oholi- 18
bamah Esau's wife; duke Jeush, duke Jalam, duke Korah:
these are the dukes that came of Oholibamah the daughter of Anah, Esau's wife. These are the sons of Esau, and 19
these are their dukes: the same is Edom.

These are the sons of Seir the Horite, the inhabitants 20
of the land; Lotan and Shobal and Zibeon and Anah, and 21
Dishon and Ezer and Dishan: these are the dukes that

---

12. **Amalek.** The tribe of Bedouin marauders who often came
into conflict with the Israelites, Exod. xvii. 8 ff.; Deut. xxv.
17; 1 Sam. xv. 2 ff. They are represented here as not genuine
Edomites.

15. **dukes.** Better 'chieftains,' i.e. heads of clans. The title
seems to be an Edomite one, cf. Exod. xv. 15, although it is
afterwards used of a Jewish governor, Zech. ix. 7, xii. 5, 6.

20. **sons of Seir.** Elsewhere Seir is used only of the land.

came of the Horites, the children of Seir in the land of
22 Edom. And the children of Lotan were Hori and Hemam;
23 and Lotan's sister was Timna. And these are the children
of Shobal; Alvan and Manahath and Ebal, Shepho and
24 Onam. And these are the children of Zibeon; Aiah and
Anah: this is Anah who found the hot springs in the
25 wilderness, as he fed the asses of Zibeon his father. And
these are the children of Anah; Dishon and Oholibamah
26 the daughter of Anah. And these are the children of
Dishon; Hemdan and Eshban and Ithran and Cheran.
27 These are the children of Ezer; Bilhan and Zaavan and
28 Akan. These are the children of Dishan; Uz and Aran.
29 These are the dukes that came of the Horites; duke Lotan,
30 duke Shobal, duke Zibeon, duke Anah, duke Dishon, duke
Ezer, duke Dishan: these are the dukes that came of the
Horites, according to their dukes in the land of Seir.

31   And these are the kings that reigned in the land of Edom,
before there reigned any king over the children of Israel.
32 And Bela the son of Beor reigned in Edom; and the name
33 of his city was Dinhabah. And Bela died, and Jobab the
34 son of Zerah of Bozrah reigned in his stead. And Jobab
died, and Husham of the land of the Temanites reigned
35 in his stead. And Husham died, and Hadad the son of
Bedad, who smote Midian in the field of Moab, reigned
36 in his stead: and the name of his city was Avith. And
Hadad died, and Samlah of Masrekah reigned in his stead.

---

24. the hot springs. Possibly those of Kallirhoe, E. of the
Dead Sea. Some versions render 'mules.'

31. before there reigned any king. The writer is evidently
living in the times of the Hebrew monarchy. The Edomite kings,
of whom eight are mentioned here, were evidently not hereditary
monarchs as none is succeeded by his son.

32. Bela the son of Beor. The name is curiously like that of
Balaam the son of Beor (Numb. xxii. 5).

33. Bozrah: an Edomite town of some importance 20 miles
S.E. of the Dead Sea, cf. Isa. lxiii. 1; Amos i. 12.

And Samlah died, and Shaul of Rehoboth by the River 37
reigned in his stead. And Shaul died, and Baal-hanan the 38
son of Achbor reigned in his stead. And Baal-hanan the 39
son of Achbor died, and Hadar reigned in his stead: and
the name of his city was Pau; and his wife's name was
Mehetabel, the daughter of Matred, the daughter of Me-
zahab. And these are the names of the dukes that came of 40
Esau, according to their families, after their places, by their
names; duke Timnah, duke Alvah, duke Jetheth; duke 41
Oholibamah, duke Elah, duke Pinon; duke Kenaz, duke 42
Teman, duke Mibzar; duke Magdiel, duke Iram: these 43
be the dukes of Edom, according to their habitations in
the land of their possession. This is Esau the father of
the Edomites.

xxxvii., xxxix.-l. *The story of Joseph and his brethren.*
xxxvii. *Joseph sold into Egypt.*

And Jacob dwelt in the land of his father's sojournings, **37**
in the land of Canaan. These are the generations of Jacob. **2**

---

37. the River. R.V. by printing with a capital understands
this to be the Euphrates. But the Euphrates was a long way off
and the river meant may be the Wady el Arish, the 'River of
Egypt.' The Rehoboth mentioned here is probably not the same
as that which occurs in xxvi. 22.

38. Baal-hanan: a variant of Hannibal = Baal is gracious.
The worship of Baal was widespread in Canaan.

41. duke Oholibamah. The name (= my tent is a high place)
is also that of one of Esau's wives.

xxxvii., xxxix.-l. We enter here upon the most detailed
story in Genesis. There are indications in places that two strands
have been woven together, as for instance, in the account in
xxxvii. of how Joseph was brought to Egypt (compare *v.* 22 with
v. 26 and *v.* 25 with *v.* 28), but for the most part the narrative
is simple and straightforward and very human. The moral lessons are not obtruded, but they are unmistakeable.

xxxvii. 2. These are the generations: a formula in P which
usually begins a new section, but occasionally ends it (ii. 4). It
is inserted here to shew that the narrative will now deal not so
much with Jacob himself, as with his descendants.

Joseph, being seventeen years old, was feeding the flock
with his brethren; and he was a lad with the sons of Bilhah,
and with the sons of Zilpah, his father's wives: and Joseph
3 brought the evil report of them unto their father. Now
Israel loved Joseph more than all his children, because he
was the son of his old age: and he made him a coat of
4 many colours. And his brethren saw that their father loved
him more than all his brethren; and they hated him, and
5 could not speak peaceably unto him. And Joseph dreamed
a dream, and he told it to his brethren: and they hated
6 him yet the more. And he said unto them, Hear, I pray
7 you, this dream which I have dreamed: for, behold, we
were binding sheaves in the field, and, lo, my sheaf arose,
and also stood upright; and, behold, your sheaves came
8 round about, and made obeisance to my sheaf. And his
brethren said to him, Shalt thou indeed reign over us? or
shalt thou indeed have dominion over us? And they hated
9 him yet the more for his dreams, and for his words. And
he dreamed yet another dream, and told it to his brethren,
and said, Behold, I have dreamed yet a dream; and,
behold, the sun and the moon and eleven stars made

---

sons of Bilhah...Zilpah: i.e. Dan and Naphtali, Gad and
Asher. Nothing is said here about the sons of Leah. Possibly
they are omitted so as not to be included in the 'evil report.'

3. a coat of many colours. The same expression in 2 Sam.
xiii. 18. The translation is taken from the Greek and Latin Versions, but the literal meaning is 'coat of extremities' i.e. reaching to
hands and feet. Hence R.V. marg. 'a long garment with sleeves.'

4. they hated him. As so often jealousy led on to hatred.
The brothers' hatred forms an effective contrast to the father's
love.

5. dreamed a dream. The narrative of Joseph abounds in
dreams, cf. xl. 8 ff., xli. 1 ff. Such passages are assigned to E.
The dreams come usually in pairs. Joseph's dreams deal naturally with familiar things: the harvest and the heavenly bodies.
Possibly the family were all busy with harvest at the time.

7. binding sheaves. The Eastern sheaf is usually little more
than the heads of corn. The straw was often burned as it stood.

obeisance to me. And he told it to his father, and to his 10
brethren; and his father rebuked him, and said unto him,
What is this dream that thou hast dreamed? Shall I and
thy mother and thy brethren indeed come to bow down
ourselves to thee to the earth? And his brethren envied 11
him; but his father kept the saying in mind. And his 12
brethren went to feed their father's flock in Shechem. And 13
Israel said unto Joseph, Do not thy brethren feed the flock
in Shechem? come, and I will send thee unto them. And 14
he said to him, Here am I. And he said to him, Go
now, see whether it be well with thy brethren, and well with
the flock; and bring me word again. So he sent him out of
the vale of Hebron, and he came to Shechem. And a 15
certain man found him, and, behold, he was wandering
in the field: and the man asked him, saying, What seekest
thou? And he said, I seek my brethren: tell me, I pray 16
thee, where they are feeding *the flock*. And the man said, 17
They are departed hence: for I heard them say, Let us
go to Dothan. And Joseph went after his brethren, and
found them in Dothan. And they saw him afar off, and 18
before he came near unto them, they conspired against
him to slay him. And they said one to another, Behold, 19
this dreamer cometh. Come now therefore, and let us slay 20

10. **thy mother.** Rachel is apparently still alive, though her
death has been related in xxxv. 19.

11. **kept the saying in mind.** Like the Virgin Mary (Luke
ii. 51), he was destined to recall the words later on.

12. **Shechem.** There is no reference to the story told in
xxxiv. 25 ff. The country round Shechem was famous for its
pastures.

14. **see whether it be well....** David was sent on a similar
errand, 1 Sam. xvii. 17 f.

17. **Dothan:** about 15 miles further north than Shechem.
This was later the scene of Elisha's deliverance, 2 Kings vi. 13-
18.

19. **this dreamer:** lit. 'this lord of dreams.' The brothers
contemptuously refer to his visions of future greatness (*v.* 8) as
being as unsubstantial as dreams.

him, and cast him into one of the pits, and we will say, An
evil beast hath devoured him: and we shall see what will
21 become of his dreams. And Reuben heard it, and delivered
him out of their hand; and said, Let us not take his life.
22 And Reuben said unto them, Shed no blood; cast him into
this pit that is in the wilderness, but lay no hand upon
him: that he might deliver him out of their hand, to re-
23 store him to his father. And it came to pass, when Joseph
was come unto his brethren, that they stript Joseph of his
24 coat, the coat of many colours that was on him; and they
took him, and cast him into the pit: and the pit was empty,
25 there was no water in it. And they sat down to eat bread:
and they lifted up their eyes and looked, and, behold, a
travelling company of Ishmaelites came from Gilead, with
their camels bearing spicery and balm and myrrh, going
26 to carry it down to Egypt. And Judah said unto his brethren, What profit is it if we slay our brother and conceal

---

20. one of the pits. It is said that cisterns are specially common round Dothan, and are shaped something like a bottle with
a narrow mouth.

21. Reuben heard it. Many scholars suppose that 'Reuben'
in this verse has been substituted for 'Judah' and that the sequel
of this verse is *vv.* 26 f. In the source known as J. Judah seems
to be Joseph's deliverer, whereas in E. Reuben plays this rôle.

22. Shed no blood. Reuben has occasion to refer to these
words of his later on at a very anxious moment, xlii. 22.

23. they stript Joseph of his coat. A very human touch.
The coat had always been hateful to them. Cf. *vv.* 3, 4.

25. a travelling company: cf. Isa. xxi. 13. It seems a pity
that R.V. did not use the ordinary word 'caravan' as in Job vi.
18 f. The caravan route from Gilead crossed the Jordan near
Beth-shan, and passed through Jezreel and Dothan.

spicery: rather 'aromatic gums.'

balm: a noted product of Gilead, cf. Jer. viii. 22.

myrrh: not the ordinary word for myrrh, but *ladanum* the
gum of the cistus rose. The articles which the camels carried
would be such as would be used in embalming. It is a touch of
irony that Joseph should enter the land of his future greatness as
an unconsidered addition to a bale of apothecary's goods.

his blood? Come, and let us sell him to the Ishmaelites, 27
and let not our hand be upon him; for he is our brother,
our flesh. And his brethren hearkened unto him. And 28
there passed by Midianites, merchantmen; and they drew
and lifted up Joseph out of the pit, and sold Joseph to the
Ishmaelites for twenty pieces of silver. And they brought
Joseph into Egypt. And Reuben returned unto the pit; 29
and, behold, Joseph was not in the pit; and he rent his
clothes. And he returned unto his brethren, and said, The 30
child is not; and I, whither shall I go? And they took 31
Joseph's coat, and killed a he-goat, and dipped the coat in
the blood; and they sent the coat of many colours, and 32
they brought it to their father; and said, This have we
found: know now whether it be thy son's coat or not.
And he knew it, and said, It is my son's coat; an evil beast 33
hath devoured him; Joseph is without doubt torn in pieces.
And Jacob rent his garments, and put sackcloth upon his 34
loins, and mourned for his son many days. And all his 35
sons and all his daughters rose up to comfort him; but he

---

28. Midianites. Two traditions seem to be blended in this
verse. According to one (E) Midianites come and take Joseph
out of the pit and carry him off: according to the other (J) the
brothers sell him to the Ishmaelites. So in *v.* 26 Judah takes
the place of Reuben (*v.* 21).

twenty pieces of silver. An adult slave was apparently priced
at 30 pieces (Exod. xxi. 32).

32. brought it to their father. A touch of pathos that the
coat which was the outward symbol of Jacob's love for Joseph,
should be chosen as the medium by which the bad news should
be brought.

33. Jacob in his anguish does not stop to enquire how the evil
beast (presumably a lion) could have devoured everything except
the coat. The sons deceive Jacob quite as successfully as he had
deceived his father.

34. put sackcloth upon his loins. The first mention of a
common mourning custom: cf. 2 Sam. iii. 31; Joel i. 13, etc.

35. all his daughters. We have not heard of any daughters
except Dinah.

refused to be comforted; and he said, For I will go down
to the grave to my son mourning. And his father wept
36 for him. And the Midianites sold him into Egypt unto
Potiphar, an officer of Pharaoh's, the captain of the guard.

xxxviii. *The story of Judah and Tamar.*

38   And it came to pass at that time, that Judah went down
from his brethren, and turned in to a certain Adullamite,
2 whose name was Hirah. And Judah saw there a daughter
of a certain Canaanite whose name was Shua; and he
3 took her, and went in unto her. And she conceived, and
4 bare a son; and he called his name Er. And she conceived
again, and bare a son; and she called his name Onan.
5 And she yet again bare a son, and called his name Shelah:

---

to the grave: i.e. to Sheol. It is doubtful whether Jacob
looked forward to any reunion with his son there, for life in
Sheol was usually regarded as a shadowy unsubstantial existence.

36. Potiphar. The word is said to be a genuine Egyptian one,
and to mean 'the gift of [the god] Ra.'

captain of the guard: lit. 'of the slaughterers.' The same
title is applied to the Babylonian officer in 2 Kings xxv. 8 ff.
Robertson Smith supposes that the king's bodyguard were origin-
ally the royal butchers. But it seems not improbable that a
genuine Babylonian word underlies the word rendered 'slaughterers.' The tablets found at Tel-el-Amarna dating from the
14th cent. B.C. shew that the Babylonian language was known at
any rate in official circles in Egypt.

xxxviii. The story interrupts the history of Joseph, and what-
ever interest it possesses is mainly in connection with tribal
legends. It brings out clearly the *levirate law* by which a man
was bound to act as husband to the wife of his deceased brother
(cf. Deut. xxv. 5; Matt. xxii. 24), and shews that the penalty for
adultery for a woman was death by burning (cf. Lev. xxi. 9, of the
daughter of a priest, and contrast Deut. xxii. 22; John viii. 5).

It may be that underlying the story is a tradition of tribal
relationship, shewing how the Israelites intermarried with the
Canaanites, the original inhabitants of the land.

1. Adullamite. Adullam lies about 17 miles S.W. of Jerusalem.
In Josh. xii. 15 it has a king. The cave of Adullam was one of
David's refuges, 1 Sam. xxii. 1,

and he was at Chezib, when she bare him. And Judah 6
took a wife for Er his firstborn, and her name was Tamar.
And Er, Judah's firstborn, was wicked in the sight of the 7
LORD; and the LORD slew him. And Judah said unto 8
Onan, Go in unto thy brother's wife, and perform the duty
of an husband's brother unto her, and raise up seed to thy
brother. And Onan knew that the seed should not be his; 9
and it came to pass, when he went in unto his brother's
wife, that he spilled it on the ground, lest he should give
seed to his brother. And the thing which he did was evil 10
in the sight of the LORD: and he slew him also. Then said 11
Judah to Tamar his daughter in law, Remain a widow in
thy father's house, till Shelah my son be grown up: for he
said, Lest he also die, like his brethren. And Tamar went
and dwelt in her father's house. And in process of time 12
Shua's daughter, the wife of Judah, died; and Judah was
comforted, and went up unto his sheepshearers to Timnah,
he and his friend Hirah the Adullamite. And it was told 13
Tamar, saying, Behold, thy father in law goeth up to
Timnah to shear his sheep. And she put off from her the 14
garments of her widowhood, and covered herself with her
veil, and wrapped herself, and sat in the gate of Enaim,
which is by the way to Timnah; for she saw that Shelah
was grown up, and she was not given unto him to wife.
When Judah saw her, he thought her to be an harlot; for 15
she had covered her face. And he turned unto her by the 16

---

6. Judah took a wife for Er. It was the father's duty to find
a wife for his son: cf. xxiv. 4, xxxiv. 4.

11. Remain a widow in thy father's house. A widow without children returns to her own people, cf. Ruth i. 8.

12. was comforted. We should say 'went out of mourning.'

Timnah. About 8 miles W. of Beth-lehem. There was
another Timnah in the Philistine country mentioned in the story
of Samson, Judg. xiv. 1, 2, 5.

14. covered herself with her veil. The garb of women who
dedicated themselves to impurity in the name of religion.

way, and said, Go to, I pray thee, let me come in unto
thee : for he knew not that she was his daughter in law.
And she said, What wilt thou give me, that thou mayest
17 come in unto me? And he said, I will send thee a kid of
the goats from the flock. And she said, Wilt thou give me
18 a pledge, till thou send it? And he said, What pledge shall
I give thee? And she said, Thy signet and thy cord, and
thy staff that is in thine hand. And he gave them to her,
19 and came in unto her, and she conceived by him. And
she arose, and went away, and put off her veil from her,
20 and put on the garments of her widowhood. And Judah
sent the kid of the goats by the hand of his friend the
Adullamite, to receive the pledge from the woman's hand :
21 but he found her not. Then he asked the men of her place,
saying, Where is the harlot, that was at Enaim by the way
22 side? And they said, There hath been no harlot here. And
he returned to Judah, and said, I have not found her ; and
also the men of the place said, There hath been no harlot
23 here. And Judah said, Let her take it to her, lest we be
put to shame: behold, I sent this kid, and thou hast not
24 found her. And it came to pass about three months after,
that it was told Judah, saying, Tamar thy daughter in law
hath played the harlot; and moreover, behold, she is with
child by whoredom. And Judah said, Bring her forth, and
25 let her be burnt. When she was brought forth, she sent
to her father in law, saying, By the man, whose these are,
am I with child: and she said, Discern, I pray thee,
whose are these, the signet, and the cords, and the staff.
26 And Judah acknowledged them, and said, She is more

---

18. Thy signet. The signet ring could be worn on a cord
suspended round the neck.

24. let her be burnt. Judah as head of the family has the
power of life and death.

26. more righteous. Judah acknowledges his fault in not
carrying out the provisions of the levirate law.

righteous than I ; forasmuch as I gave her not to Shelah
my son. And he knew her again no more. And it came to 27
pass in the time of her travail, that, behold, twins were in
her womb. And it came to pass, when she travailed, that 28
one put out a hand : and the midwife took and bound upon
his hand a scarlet thread, saying, This came out first. And 29
it came to pass, as he drew back his hand, that, behold,
his brother came out : and she said, Wherefore hast thou
made a breach for thyself? therefore his name was called
Perez. And afterward came out his brother, that had the 30
scarlet thread upon his hand : and his name was called
Zerah.

xxxix. *Joseph falls into disgrace and is put in prison.*

And Joseph was brought down to Egypt; and Potiphar, **39**
an officer of Pharaoh's, the captain of the guard, an Egyptian, bought him of the hand of the Ishmaelites, which had
brought him down thither. And the LORD was with 2
Joseph, and he was a prosperous man ; and he was in the
house of his master the Egyptian. And his master saw 3
that the LORD was with him, and that the LORD made all
that he did to prosper in his hand. And Joseph found 4
grace in his sight, and he ministered unto him: and he
made him overseer over his house, and all that he had he

---

xxxix. The narrative is picked up from xxxvii. 36. Some
years must be supposed to have elapsed before the second great
change in Joseph's fortune which led him to an unjust punishment. The story of the false accusation brought against him by
Potiphar's wife is in many respects closely parallel to an Egyptian
story known as the Tale of Two Brothers which is said to have
been written for Seti II (c. 1210 B.C.). The two brothers are
Anpu and Bata, and Anpu's wife makes a false accusation against
Bata to her husband, who attempts to kill his brother. But in
the end the truth comes out, and Bata is justified, while the false
wife is put to death.
4. overseer over his house : i.e. his trusted steward, something like Eliezer, xv. 2 : cf. Luke xii. 42.

5 put into his hand. And it came to pass from the time that
he made him overseer in his house, and over all that he
had, that the LORD blessed the Egyptian's house for
Joseph's sake; and the blessing of the LORD was upon all
6 that he had, in the house and in the field. And he left all
that he had in Joseph's hand; and he knew not aught
that was with him, save the bread which he did eat. And
7 Joseph was comely, and well favoured. And it came to
pass after these things, that his master's wife cast her eyes
8 upon Joseph; and she said, Lie with me. But he refused,
and said unto his master's wife, Behold, my master knoweth not what is with me in the house, and he hath put all
9 that he hath into my hand; there is none greater in this
house than I; neither hath he kept back any thing from
me but thee, because thou art his wife: how then can I
10 do this great wickedness, and sin against God? And it
came to pass, as she spake to Joseph day by day, that he
hearkened not unto her, to lie by her, *or* to be with her.
11 And it came to pass about this time, that he went into the
house to do his work; and there was none of the men of
12 the house there within. And she caught him by his garment, saying, Lie with me: and he left his garment in
13 her hand, and fled, and got him out. And it came to pass,
when she saw that he had left his garment in her hand,
14 and was fled forth, that she called unto the men of her

---

6. save the bread. The Egyptians seem to have been almost
as particular as the modern Brahmins about their food, and Joseph
being a foreigner would be ceremonially unclean: cf. xliii. 32.

8, 9. Joseph is helped to repel the temptation by two considera-
tions: (i) the sense of his master's trust, (ii) his duty towards
God. It throws an interesting light on his character.

10. day by day. The temptation is at first a sudden one, then
it becomes like a gradual siege. But Joseph is strong enough in
his integrity to resist both kinds of trial.

12. he left his garment: i.e. the loose outer robe that would
easily slip off: cf. Mark xiv. 51 f.

house, and spake unto them, saying, See, he hath brought
in an Hebrew unto us to mock us; he came in unto me to
lie with me, and I cried with a loud voice: and it came to 15
pass, when he heard that I lifted up my voice and cried,
that he left his garment by me, and fled, and got him out.
And she laid up his garment by her, until his master came 16
home. And she spake unto him according to these words, 17
saying, The Hebrew servant, which thou hast brought
unto us, came in unto me to mock me: and it came to 18
pass, as I lifted up my voice and cried, that he left his
garment by me, and fled out. And it came to pass, when 19
his master heard the words of his wife, which she spake
unto him, saying, After this manner did thy servant to me;
that his wrath was kindled. And Joseph's master took 20
him, and put him into the prison, the place where the
king's prisoners were bound: and he was there in the
prison. But the LORD was with Joseph, and shewed kind- 21
ness unto him, and gave him favour in the sight of the
keeper of the prison. And the keeper of the prison com- 22
mitted to Joseph's hand all the prisoners that were in the
prison; and whatsoever they did there, he was the doer
of it. The keeper of the prison looked not to any thing 23
that was under his hand, because the LORD was with him;
and that which he did, the LORD made it to prosper.

---

14. an Hebrew. The word is generally used by foreigners,
xli. 12, or when speaking to foreigners, xl. 15.

to mock us. She implies that the other women in the house
would be in danger.

20. into the prison. One would have expected Joseph to be
put to death, but possibly his master remembered how useful he
had been to him.

the king's prisoners. Apparently it was not the common
prison, but the one reserved for state offenders. If so it is a
tribute to the position which Joseph had won for himself.

21. the LORD was with Joseph: cf. *v.* 2. The words explain
why Joseph in each case was able to meet his special troubles,
and also why he so quickly gained the confidence of those over
him. It was characteristic of Joseph that every one trusted him.

xl. *Joseph interprets the dreams of the butler and baker.*

40   And it came to pass after these things, that the butler of the king of Egypt and his baker offended their lord the 2 king of Egypt. And Pharaoh was wroth against his two officers, against the chief of the butlers, and against the 3 chief of the bakers. And he put them in ward in the house of the captain of the guard, into the prison, the place 4 where Joseph was bound. And the captain of the guard charged Joseph with them, and he ministered unto them: 5 and they continued a season in ward. And they dreamed a dream both of them, each man his dream, in one night, each man according to the interpretation of his dream, the butler and the baker of the king of Egypt, which were 6 bound in the prison. And Joseph came in unto them in the morning, and saw them, and, behold, they were sad. 7 And he asked Pharaoh's officers that were with him in ward in his master's house, saying, Wherefore look ye so 8 sadly to-day? And they said unto him, We have dreamed a dream, and there is none that can interpret it. And Joseph said unto them, Do not interpretations belong to 9 God? tell it me, I pray you. And the chief butler told his dream to Joseph, and said to him, In my dream, behold, 10 a vine was before me; and in the vine were three branches:

---

xl. 1. after these things. The words mark the beginning of a new section, cf. xv. 1, xxii. 1.

butler...baker. These are to be regarded as high officials.

3. in ward: i.e. under arrest. The latter part of the verse 'into the prison...bound' preserves a different tradition, or is perhaps an editorial addition. See *v.* 15.

6. they were sad. They felt sure that the dreams had a meaning, and being in prison they were not able to consult the professional interpreters of dreams.

8. Do not interpretations belong to God? Compare Daniel's words in Dan. ii. 28. Joseph means that dreams may be interpreted only by Divine revelation, not by human skill. At the same time he implies that God will shew him the interpretation.

10. In a dream events are foreshortened, and the process of

and it was as though it budded, *and* its blossoms shot forth ; *and* the clusters thereof brought forth ripe grapes: and Pharaoh's cup was in my hand; and I took the grapes, 11 and pressed them into Pharaoh's cup, and I gave the cup into Pharaoh's hand. And Joseph said unto him, This is 12 the interpretation of it : the three branches are three days; within yet three days shall Pharaoh lift up thine head, 13 and restore thee unto thine office : and thou shalt give Pharaoh's cup into his hand, after the former manner when thou wast his butler. But have me in thy remem- 14 brance when it shall be well with thee, and shew kindness, I pray thee, unto me, and make mention of me unto Pharaoh, and bring me out of this house : for indeed I 15 was stolen away out of the land of the Hebrews : and here also have I done nothing that they should put me into the dungeon. When the chief baker saw that the interpreta- 16 tion was good, he said unto Joseph, I also was in my dream, and, behold, three baskets of white bread were on my head : and in the uppermost basket there was of all 17 manner of bakemeats for Pharaoh ; and the birds did eat them out of the basket upon my head. And Joseph an- 18

---

months occupy but a few seconds. So also the whole process of wine making is compressed into the squeezing of the grapes into Pharaoh's cup.

13. lift up thine head: in the technical meaning of 'restore to honour': cf. 2 Kings xxv. 27.

15. I was stolen away. Perhaps referring to E's account that the Midianites had carried him off out of the pit. See note on xxxvii. 28.

and here...dungeon. Possibly another editorial addition to bring the story into connection with the last chapter. 'Dungeon' is literally 'pit.' It is the same word (though with different meaning) as that used in xxxvii. 24.

16. baskets of white bread. The bread of ordinary people would be brown barley bread.

17. the birds: possibly the kites which are very bold, and are always ready to swoop down and carry off food. The baker with the baskets poised on his head would be powerless to stop them, so the dream would be a typical nightmare.

swered and said, This is the interpretation thereof : the
19 three baskets are three days; within yet three days shall
Pharaoh lift up thy head from off thee, and shall hang
thee on a tree; and the birds shall eat thy flesh from off
20 thee. And it came to pass the third day, which was
Pharaoh's birthday, that he made a feast unto all his
servants : and he lifted up the head of the chief butler
21 and the head of the chief baker among his servants. And
he restored the chief butler unto his butlership again;
22 and he gave the cup into Pharaoh's hand : but he hanged
23 the chief baker : as Joseph had interpreted to them. Yet
did not the chief butler remember Joseph, but forgat
him.

xli. *Joseph interprets Pharaoh's dreams and becomes chief minister of Egypt.*

41 And it came to pass at the end of two full years, that
Pharaoh dreamed : and, behold, he stood by the river.
2 And, behold, there came up out of the river seven kine,
well favoured and fatfleshed; and they fed in the reed-
3 grass. And, behold, seven other kine came up after them
out of the river, ill favoured and leanfleshed; and stood
4 by the other kine upon the brink of the river. And the ill

---

19. lift up thy head. A touch of grim humour, the verb being
used in a very different sense to that found in *v.* 13.

the birds shall eat thy flesh. The Egyptians had a special
horror of the mangling of a corpse as precluding the hope of a
life after death. The choice morsels in the dream turned out to
be the baker's flesh.

23. but forgat him. Another trial to Joseph's patience and
faith—two years of hope deferred. It is also another very human
touch.

xli. 1. by the river : i.e. the Nile. The word is said to be an
Egyptian one, as is also that for 'reed-grass' in *v.* 2. In Dan.
xii. 5 it is used of the Tigris.

2. seven kine. These would probably be the *gemoos*, or water
buffaloes, which love to stand in the river with only the nose above
water.

favoured and leanfleshed kine did eat up the seven well
favoured and fat kine. So Pharaoh awoke. And he slept 5
and dreamed a second time : and, behold, seven ears of
corn came up upon one stalk, rank and good. And, behold, 6
seven ears, thin and blasted with the east wind, sprung
up after them. And the thin ears swallowed up the seven 7
rank and full ears. And Pharaoh awoke, and, behold, it
was a dream. And it came to pass in the morning that 8
his spirit was troubled ; and he sent and called for all the
magicians of Egypt, and all the wise men thereof : and
Pharaoh told them his dream ; but there was none that
could interpret them unto Pharaoh. Then spake the chief 9
butler unto Pharaoh, saying, I do remember my faults this
day : Pharaoh was wroth with his servants, and put me in 10
ward in the house of the captain of the guard, me and the
chief baker : and we dreamed a dream in one night, I and 11
he ; we dreamed each man according to the interpretation
of his dream. And there was with us there a young man, 12
an Hebrew, servant to the captain of the guard ; and we
told him, and he interpreted to us our dreams ; to each
man according to his dream he did interpret. And it came 13

---

4. did eat up. This, of course, would never happen in actual
life, but it is in keeping with the character of a dream.

6. blasted with the east wind. In Egypt the prevailing wind
is north which brings welcome relief from the heat ; when it blows
from the east it is often laden with sand, and parches everything.
It is often called *shirocco* (=east) or sometimes (from the fact
that it may continue for 50 days) *hamsîn* (=fifty).

8. magicians. The same word found in Exod. vii.-ix., in
connection with the plagues, and in Daniel ii. 2. A class of professional men represented in inscriptions with writing materials
in their hands and a pen on their temples.

9. remember. Rather 'confess.'

11. according to the interpretation : i.e. with the interpretation differing in each case, cf. xl. 5.

12. servant to the captain of the guard. The butler does
not seem to speak of Joseph as a prisoner. See note on xl. 3.
But in *v.* 14 he is 'in the dungeon.'

to pass, as he interpreted to us, so it was ; me he restored
14 unto mine office, and him he hanged. Then Pharaoh sent
and called Joseph, and they brought him hastily out of
the dungeon : and he shaved himself, and changed his
15 raiment, and came in unto Pharaoh. And Pharaoh said
unto Joseph, I have dreamed a dream, and there is none
that can interpret it : and I have heard say of thee, that
16 when thou hearest a dream thou canst interpret it. And
Joseph answered Pharaoh, saying, It is not in me : God
17 shall give Pharaoh an answer of peace. And Pharaoh
spake unto Joseph, In my dream, behold, I stood upon
18 the brink of the river : and, behold, there came up out of
the river seven kine, fatfleshed and well favoured ; and
19 they fed in the reed-grass : and, behold, seven other kine
came up after them, poor and very ill favoured and leanfleshed, such as I never saw in all the land of Egypt for
20 badness : and the lean and ill favoured kine did eat up
21 the first seven fat kine : and when they had eaten them
up, it could not be known that they had eaten them ; but
they were still ill favoured, as at the beginning. So I
22 awoke. And I saw in my dream, and, behold, seven ears
23 came up upon one stalk, full and good : and, behold, seven
ears, withered, thin, *and* blasted with the east wind, sprung
24 up after them : and the thin ears swallowed up the seven
good ears : and I told it unto the magicians ; but there
25 was none that could declare it to me. And Joseph said
unto Pharaoh, The dream of Pharaoh is one : what God
26 is about to do he hath declared unto Pharaoh. The seven

---

13. me he restored. The chief butler gives the gist of Joseph's
interpretation of the dreams.

14. he shaved himself. The Egyptians were very particular
about personal cleanliness and shaved both head and face. They
are said to have used razors made of bronze.

16. It is not in me. One word in Hebrew, 'Not I.' Found
again in xiv. 24.

an answer of peace : i.e. an answer that will bring good.

good kine are seven years; and the seven good ears are
seven years: the dream is one. And the seven lean and 27
ill favoured kine that came up after them are seven years,
and also the seven empty ears blasted with the east wind;
they shall be seven years of famine. That is the thing 28
which I spake unto Pharaoh : what God is about to do he
hath shewed unto Pharaoh. Behold, there come seven 29
years of great plenty throughout all the land of Egypt:
and there shall arise after them seven years of famine; 30
and all the plenty shall be forgotten in the land of Egypt;
and the famine shall consume the land; and the plenty 31
shall not be known in the land by reason of that famine
which followeth ; for it shall be very grievous. And for 32
that the dream was doubled unto Pharaoh twice, it is
because the thing is established by God, and God will
shortly bring it to pass. Now therefore let Pharaoh look 33
out a man discreet and wise, and set him over the land of
Egypt. Let Pharaoh do *this*, and let him appoint over- 34
seers over the land, and take up the fifth part of the land
of Egypt in the seven plenteous years. And let them 35
gather all the food of these good years that come, and lay
up corn under the hand of Pharaoh for food in the cities,

---

32. doubled. It is noticeable that in the story of Joseph
dreams generally come in pairs: cf. xxxvii. 6-9, xl. 9-17.
Joseph sees in the repetition an indication that the event sig-
nified is (*a*) certain, (*b*) imminent.

33, 34. Joseph devises a plan on the spot to meet the situation
that is about to arise. He advises the appointment of one responsible head official to be assisted by local administrators,
whose work it should be to collect together, whether by pur-
chase or as a tax, a fifth of the corn grown during the seven good
years. So bounteous was the harvest apparently that the grain
thus collected sufficed to tide over the seven years of famine.
For the number five in connection with Egypt cf. xliii. 34, xlv. 22,
xlvii. 24.

35. let them gather all the food. The important cities in
Egypt had state granaries, the corn tax being paid in kind.

36 and let them keep it. And the food shall be for a store to
the land against the seven years of famine, which shall be
in the land of Egypt; that the land perish not through
37 the famine. And the thing was good in the eyes of Pharaoh,
38 and in the eyes of all his servants. And Pharaoh said unto
his servants, Can we find such a one as this, a man in
39 whom the spirit of God is? And Pharaoh said unto Joseph,
Forasmuch as God hath shewed thee all this, there is
40 none so discreet and wise as thou: thou shalt be over my
house, and according unto thy word shall all my people
be ruled: only in the throne will I be greater than thou.
41 And Pharaoh said unto Joseph, See, I have set thee over
42 all the land of Egypt. And Pharaoh took off his signet
ring from his hand, and put it upon Joseph's hand, and
arrayed him in vestures of fine linen, and put a gold chain
43 about his neck; and he made him to ride in the second
chariot which he had; and they cried before him, Bow
the knee: and he set him over all the land of Egypt.
44 And Pharaoh said unto Joseph, I am Pharaoh, and with-

---

38. in whom the spirit of God is. A striking phrase in the
mouth of Pharaoh. A similar expression is used by Belshazzar of
Daniel (Dan. v. 14). The Hebrews regarded all special gifts
of art or skill or strength as due to the spirit of God, cf. Exod.
xxxi. 3; Judg. xiv. 19, etc. Compare St Paul's phrase 'the mani-
festation of the Spirit' (1 Cor. xii. 7).

42. his signet ring. With it the royal decrees would be sealed.
It is said that the keeper of the seal was the king's deputy.

fine linen. White linen robes were regularly worn by Egyptians
of high rank.

a gold chain. A specially Egyptian form of decoration.

43. Bow the knee. The meaning is quite uncertain. Probably
the word is more or less transliterated from the Egyptian. 'Thy
command is our desire' has been suggested as a translation of the
Egyptian. Or it may be connected with a Babylonian word
meaning Grand Vizier, Babylonian being the diplomatic language
of the time. One of the Targums renders 'this is the father of the
king,' but this translation seems to rest on a queer mixture of
Hebrew and Latin.

out thee shall no man lift up his hand or his foot in all
the land of Egypt. And Pharaoh called Joseph's name 45
Zaphenath-paneah; and he gave him to wife Asenath the
daughter of Poti-phera priest of On. And Joseph went
out over the land of Egypt. And Joseph was thirty years 46
old when he stood before Pharaoh king of Egypt. And
Joseph went out from the presence of Pharaoh, and went
throughout all the land of Egypt. And in the seven plen- 47
teous years the earth brought forth by handfuls. And he 48
gathered up all the food of the seven years which were in
the land of Egypt, and laid up the food in the cities: the
food of the field, which was round about every city, laid
he up in the same. And Joseph laid up corn as the sand 49
of the sea, very much, until he left numbering; for it was
without number. And unto Joseph were born two sons 50
before the year of famine came, which Asenath the daughter of Poti-phera priest of On bare unto him. And Joseph 51

---

45. Zaphenath-paneah. Egyptian scholars tell us that this
means 'God speaks and he (i.e. the bearer of the title) lives.'
Jerome renders it 'Saviour of the world.' Josephus seems to treat
the word as a hybrid from Hebrew and Greek and translates 're-
vealer of secrets.'

Asenath. The word is said to mean 'belonging to Neith'
(a goddess).

priest of On. *On* is the same as Aven in Ezek. xxx. 17. The
place is better known by its Greek name of Heliopolis. It cor-
responds more with Matarieh, than with the modern Heliopolis
which is a fashionable suburb of Cairo. Here two ancient obe-
lisks stood in Joseph's day, one of which still remains in its
original position.

46. thirty years old. In xxxvii. 2 we are told that he was
17 years old at the beginning of the narrative. It was very soon
after this that he was sold into Egypt, so he had been there
12 or 13 years.

47. the earth brought forth by handfuls. The fertility of
Egypt depends almost entirely on a 'high Nile,' which floods the
country between August and October, and brings down an abun-
dance of fertilizing silt.

called the name of the firstborn Manasseh : For, *said he*,
God hath made me forget all my toil, and all my father's
52 house. And the name of the second called he Ephraim :
For God hath made me fruitful in the land of my affliction.
53 And the seven years of plenty, that was in the land of
54 Egypt, came to an end. And the seven years of famine
began to come, according as Joseph had said : and there
was famine in all lands ; but in all the land of Egypt there
55 was bread. And when all the land of Egypt was famished,
the people cried to Pharaoh for bread : and Pharaoh said
unto all the Egyptians, Go unto Joseph ; what he saith to
56 you, do. And the famine was over all the face of the earth :
and Joseph opened all the storehouses, and sold unto the
Egyptians ; and the famine was sore in the land of Egypt.
57 And all countries came into Egypt to Joseph for to buy
corn ; because the famine was sore in all the earth.

   xlii. *Joseph's brethren come to Egypt to buy corn.*

42   Now Jacob saw that there was corn in Egypt, and Jacob
said unto his sons, Why do ye look one upon another?
2 And he said, Behold, I have heard that there is corn in
Egypt : get you down thither, and buy for us from thence;

---

51. Manasseh : i.e. 'making to forget.' Now at last he was
able to trace God's good hand in his history.

all my father's house. Joseph implies that now his home-
sickness is dispelled.

52. Ephraim. A curious dual form of name connected with
the root meaning 'be fruitful.' Ephraim became the most powerful of the N. Israelite tribes.

55. what he saith to you, do. The same words were spoken
of a greater than Joseph, cf. John ii. 5.

57. all countries : an obvious exaggeration, but preparing the
way for the next chapter.

xlii. 1. look one upon another. A rare use of the word. In
2 Kings xiv. 8, 11 it denotes meeting in battle. Possibly the
brothers were taunting one another in their extremity.

2. corn. The word is not the usual one, and is found only in
these chapters and in Amos viii. 5; Neh. x. 32.

that we may live, and not die. And Joseph's ten brethren 3
went down to buy corn from Egypt. But Benjamin, Jo- 4
seph's brother, Jacob sent not with his brethren; for he
said, Lest peradventure mischief befall him. And the sons 5
of Israel came to buy among those that came: for the
famine was in the land of Canaan. And Joseph was the 6
governor over the land; he it was that sold to all the
people of the land: and Joseph's brethren came, and bowed
down themselves to him with their faces to the earth.
And Joseph saw his brethren, and he knew them, but 7
made himself strange unto them, and spake roughly with
them; and he said unto them, Whence come ye? And
they said, From the land of Canaan to buy food. And 8
Joseph knew his brethren, but they knew not him. And 9
Joseph remembered the dreams which he dreamed of them,
and said unto them, Ye are spies; to see the nakedness
of the land ye are come. And they said unto him, Nay, 10
my lord, but to buy food are thy servants come. We are 11
all one man's sons; we are true men, thy servants are no
spies. And he said unto them, Nay, but to see the naked- 12
ness of the land ye are come. And they said, We thy 13
servants are twelve brethren, the sons of one man in the
land of Canaan; and, behold, the youngest. is this day
with our father, and one is not. And Joseph said unto 14

---

4. Benjamin as being Rachel's only other son takes Joseph's
place in the father's affections.

6. **the governor**: a new title expressing paramount authority.
The same root gives the Arabic word 'Sultan.'

7. **spake roughly.** Apparently he is testing them to see if they
are worthy of forgiveness. In any case the 'rough speaking' is
necessary to the working out of the drama, but apart from that
we can hardly acquit Joseph of rather overdoing the advantage
he enjoyed over his brethren.

9. **nakedness**: i.e. 'defencelessness.' Egypt has always been
most vulnerable on the N.E. frontier. If the Hyksos were in
power at the time, their capital was at Avaris not far inside the
frontier.

them, That is it that I spake unto you, saying, Ye are
15 spies: hereby ye shall be proved: by the life of Pharaoh
ye shall not go forth hence, except your youngest brother
16 come hither. Send one of you, and let him fetch your
brother, and ye shall be bound, that your words may be
proved, whether there be truth in you: or else by the life
17 of Pharaoh surely ye are spies. And he put them all to-
18 gether into ward three days. And Joseph said unto them
19 the third day, This do, and live; for I fear God: if ye be
true men, let one of your brethren be bound in your
prison house; but go ye, carry corn for the famine of your
20 houses: and bring your youngest brother unto me; so
shall your words be verified, and ye shall not die. And
21 they did so. And they said one to another, We are verily guilty concerning our brother, in that we saw the distress of his soul, when he besought us, and we would not
22 hear; therefore is this distress come upon us. And Reuben answered them, saying, Spake I not unto you, saying,
Do not sin against the child; and ye would not hear?
23 therefore also, behold, his blood is required. And they
knew not that Joseph understood them; for there was an
24 interpreter between them. And he turned himself about
from them, and wept; and he returned to them, and

---

15. by the life of Pharaoh. A similar oath is found in an
Egyptian inscription previous to this time. The Hebrew equiva-
lent is 'As the LORD liveth.'

17. into ward: rather 'under arrest.' The word is not the
same as that used of Joseph's prison.

18. I fear God. Joseph assures his brothers that his actions
are not arbitrary, but are regulated by religious principles. Contrast xx. 11.

21. We are verily guilty. The brethren shew signs of true
penitence. Compare the prodigal's words in Luke xv. 21.

saw the distress of his soul. It had made no visible impression at the time, but their hearts were not made of stone, and
the sight of the lad's anguish had left a permanent impression.

spake to them, and took Simeon from among them, and bound him before their eyes. Then Joseph commanded 25 to fill their vessels with corn, and to restore every man's money into his sack, and to give them provision for the way: and thus was it done unto them. And they laded 26 their asses with their corn, and departed thence. And 27 as one of them opened his sack to give his ass provender in the lodging place, he espied his money; and, behold, it was in the mouth of his sack. And he said unto his 28 brethren, My money is restored; and, lo, it is even in my sack: and their heart failed them, and they turned trembling one to another, saying, What is this that God hath done unto us? And they came unto Jacob their father 29 unto the land of Canaan, and told him all that had befallen them; saying, The man, the lord of the land, spake 30 roughly with us, and took us for spies of the country. And we said unto him, We are true men; we are no spies: 31 we be twelve brethren, sons of our father; one is not, and 32 the youngest is this day with our father in the land of Canaan. And the man, the lord of the land, said unto us, 33 Hereby shall I know that ye are true men; leave one of your brethren with me, and take *corn for* the famine of your houses, and go your way: and bring your youngest 34 brother unto me: then shall I know that ye are no spies,

---

24. took Simeon: the second oldest of the brothers. Possibly Reuben was passed over because of his efforts to save Joseph (xxxvii. 22) or for the words he had just spoken (xlii. 22).

bound him before their eyes. Outwardly Joseph is stern and exacting, though inwardly he is full of pity ('turned himself... and wept').

27. the lodging place. Probably an empty rest-house provided for the use of travellers.

28. My money is restored. The other bundles of money seem to have been at the bottom of the sacks, so they were not discovered till the brothers reached home.

God hath done unto us. They feel that somehow God's hand is behind the events that have happened to them.

but that ye are true men: so will I deliver you your brother,
35 and ye shall traffick in the land. And it came to pass as
they emptied their sacks, that, behold, every man's bundle
of money was in his sack: and when they and their father
36 saw their bundles of money, they were afraid. And Jacob
their father said unto them, Me have ye bereaved of my
children: Joseph is not, and Simeon is not, and ye will
take Benjamin away: all these things are against me.
37 And Reuben spake unto his father, saying, Slay my two
sons, if I bring him not to thee: deliver him into my
38 hand, and I will bring him to thee again. And he said,
My son shall not go down with you; for his brother is
dead, and he only is left: if mischief befall him by the
way in the which ye go, then shall ye bring down my gray
hairs with sorrow to the grave.

xliii. *Joseph's brethren go down to Egypt a second time.*

43
2   And the famine was sore in the land. And it came to
pass, when they had eaten up the corn which they had
brought out of Egypt, their father said unto them, Go
3 again, buy us a little food. And Judah spake unto him,
saying, The man did solemnly protest unto us, saying, Ye
shall not see my face, except your brother be with you.
4 If thou wilt send our brother with us, we will go down
5 and buy thee food: but if thou wilt not send him, we will
not go down : for the man said unto us, Ye shall not see
6 my face, except your brother be with you. And Israel

---

36. Me have ye bereaved. The words are the expression of
an old man's petulance. In Joseph's case they were truer than he
knew.

37. Slay my two sons. Reuben's two sons are the costliest
pledges that he can offer, but it is hard to think that Jacob
would have exacted the penalty if Benjamin had not returned.

38. to the grave. Rather 'to Sheol,' cf. xxxvii. 35.

xliii. 3. Judah. In this strand of the story (J) Judah, not
Reuben, takes the lead. Compare also *v.* 8 with xlii. 37.

said, Wherefore dealt ye so ill with me, as to tell the man
whether ye had yet a brother? And they said, The man 7
asked straitly concerning ourselves, and concerning our
kindred, saying, Is your father yet alive? have ye *another*
brother? and we told him according to the tenor of these
words: could we in any wise know that he would say,
Bring your brother down? And Judah said unto Israel 8
his father, Send the lad with me, and we will arise and
go; that we may live, and not die, both we, and thou, and
also our little ones. I will be surety for him; of my hand 9
shalt thou require him: if I bring him not unto thee, and
set him before thee, then let me bear the blame for ever:
for except we had lingered, surely we had now returned a 10
second time. And their father Israel said unto them, If it 11
be so now, do this; take of the choice fruits of the land
in your vessels, and carry down the man a present, a little
balm, and a little honey, spicery and myrrh, nuts, and

---

6. Wherefore dealt ye so ill. Faced with the dilemma of
starvation or the loss of Benjamin, Jacob gives way to another
fit of petulance. There is still a distinct trace of selfishness in
his character which is accentuated by trouble. He affects to believe that the brothers care little what happens to Benjamin so
long as their own needs are provided for.

7. straitly: i.e. strictly. In xlii. 13 the brethren volunteer the
information about their family without any questions on Joseph's
part. So we seem to have here a reference to another tradition
(J) in which the conversation between Joseph and his brothers
was much more detailed.

8. our little ones. The brothers are represented as married
men with families, although we have information only about
Judah's marriage. But cf. xlii. 37.

9. let me bear the blame for ever. The same word as that
used in xxxi. 39. Judah binds both himself and his descendants
to his father's curse if he fails to bring Benjamin back.

11. the choice fruits. This meaning is probable, though not
elsewhere attested. A Targum (Jewish commentary) renders
'things praised in the land.' The catalogue of fruits includes those
which the Ishmaelites were carrying to Egypt, xxxvii. 25.

12 almonds : and take double money in your hand; and the
money that was returned in the mouth of your sacks carry
again in your hand; peradventure it was an oversight :
13 take also your brother, and arise, go again unto the man :
14 and God Almighty give you mercy before the man, that
he may release unto you your other brother and Benjamin.
And if I be bereaved of my children, I am bereaved.
15   And the men took that present, and they took double
money in their hand, and Benjamin; and rose up, and
16 went down to Egypt, and stood before Joseph. And when
Joseph saw Benjamin with them, he said to the steward
of his house, Bring the men into the house, and slay, and
make ready; for the men shall dine with me at noon.
17 And the man did as Joseph bade; and the man brought
18 the men into Joseph's house. And the men were afraid,
because they were brought into Joseph's house; and they
said, Because of the money that was returned in our sacks
at the first time are we brought in; that he may seek
occasion against us, and fall upon us, and take us for
19 bondmen, and our asses. And they came near to the
steward of Joseph's house, and they spake unto him at the

---

12. take double money. According to the later Jewish law
a thief had to restore double what he had taken (Exod. xxii. 4).
So Jacob tries to provide for the contingency that Joseph will
not regard the bringing back of the money as an oversight.

14. God Almighty. El Shaddai. So probably xlix. 25 : elsewhere found only in P, cf. xvii. 1 ; Exod. vi. 3.

give you mercy before the man. 'The man' appears to Jacob
as a grim and relentless tyrant.

if I be bereaved. Another trace of selfishness, cf. xlii. 36.

15. stood before Joseph : in his office, not in his private house.

16. slay. Among the Hebrews at any rate meat was eaten
only at a feast.

at noon. In Palestine the chief meal was in the evening.

18. the men were afraid. A natural touch, for Joseph's house
would be large and splendid, a striking contrast to their own home.
So they make their appeal to the steward before they enter (v. 19).

door of the house, and said, Oh my lord, we came indeed 20
down at the first time to buy food: and it came to pass, 21
when we came to the lodging place, that we opened our
sacks, and, behold, every man's money was in the mouth
of his sack, our money in full weight: and we have brought
it again in our hand. And other money have we brought 22
down in our hand to buy food: we know not who put our
money in our sacks. And he said, Peace be to you, fear 23
not: your God, and the God of your father, hath given
you treasure in your sacks: I had your money. And he
brought Simeon out unto them. And the man brought 24
the men into Joseph's house, and gave them water, and
they washed their feet; and he gave their asses provender.
And they made ready the present against Joseph came at 25
noon: for they heard that they should eat bread there.
And when Joseph came home, they brought him the present 26
which was in their hand into the house, and bowed down
themselves to him to the earth. And he asked them of 27
their welfare, and said, Is your father well, the old man of
whom ye spake? Is he yet alive? And they said, Thy 28
servant our father is well, he is yet alive. And they bowed
the head, and made obeisance. And he lifted up his eyes, 29

---

20. Oh my lord: introducing an appeal; cf. xliv. 18.

23. your God, and the God of your father. The steward's
words sound as though Joseph had inspired them.

I had your money. This was of course literally true.

24. they washed their feet. The usual preliminary to a meal,
cf. xviii. 4, xxiv. 32.

25. against Joseph came: i.e. in preparation for Joseph's
coming. For this use of 'against' cf. 2 Kings xvi. 11 and (in A.V.)
Exod. vii. 15.

26. bowed down themselves. Joseph's dreams were coming
true, cf. xxxvii. 6–9.

27. Is your father well...? Lit. 'is your father in peace?' Cf.
2 Sam. xx. 9. Peace, in the sense of welfare, nearly always
enters into salutations in the East.

29. he lifted up his eyes: of taking special notice, cf. xxxix. 7.

and saw Benjamin his brother, his mother's son, and said,
Is this your youngest brother, of whom ye spake unto me?
30 And he said, God be gracious unto thee, my son. And
Joseph made haste; for his bowels did yearn upon his
brother: and he sought where to weep; and he entered
31 into his chamber, and wept there. And he washed his
face, and came out; and he refrained himself, and said,
32 Set on bread. And they set on for him by himself, and
for them by themselves, and for the Egyptians, which did
eat with him, by themselves: because the Egyptians might
not eat bread with the Hebrews; for that is an abomina-
33 tion unto the Egyptians. And they sat before him, the
firstborn according to his birthright, and the youngest
according to his youth: and the men marvelled one with
34 another. And he took *and sent* messes unto them from
before him: but Benjamin's mess was five times so much
as any of theirs. And they drank, and were merry with
him.

xliv. 1–17. *Joseph's divining cup is found in Benjamin's
sack.*

44   And he commanded the steward of his house, saying,

God be gracious unto thee. Joseph speaks as one much older
than Benjamin. Notice that he does not use the sacred name, the
LORD, as is usual in the source J.

30. his bowels did yearn: an expression for strong emotion,
cf. 1 Kings iii. 26.

wept there. Joseph's is an emotional nature and tears of joy
are not uncommon in the East.

32. Joseph by virtue of his rank dines at a separate table. The
Egyptians being very exclusive in their habits refused to eat with
foreigners. It is an early instance of caste.

33. The brethren wonder at finding themselves arranged cor-
rectly according to their ages.

34. messes. These would be not platefuls, but tit-bits sent as
a mark of special favour. For 'mess' = portion (French *met*)
cf. 2 Sam. xi. 8.

were merry. Lit. 'were drunken': a strong word toned down
in meaning. Cf. John ii. 10.

Fill the men's sacks with food, as much as they can carry, and put every man's money in his sack's mouth. And put 2 my cup, the silver cup, in the sack's mouth of the youngest, and his corn money. And he did according to the word that Joseph had spoken. As soon as the morning was 3 light, the men were sent away, they and their asses. *And* 4 when they were gone out of the city, and were not yet far off, Joseph said unto his steward, Up, follow after the men ; and when thou dost overtake them, say unto them, Wherefore have ye rewarded evil for good? Is not this it in which 5 my lord drinketh, and whereby he indeed divineth? ye have done evil in so doing. And he overtook them, and he 6 spake unto them these words. And they said unto him, 7 Wherefore speaketh my lord such words as these? God forbid that thy servants should do such a thing. Behold, 8 the money, which we found in our sacks' mouths, we brought again unto thee out of the land of Canaan: how then should we steal out of thy lord's house silver or gold? With whomsoever of thy servants it be found, let him die, 9 and we also will be my lord's bondmen. And he said, Now 10 also let it be according unto your words : he with whom it is found shall be my bondman ; and ye shall be blame-less. Then they hasted, and took down every man his 11

---

xliv. 4. The 'reversal of fortune' is very effective. Just as the brothers are congratulating themselves that all had gone well with them they are plunged again into desperate danger.

5. whereby he indeed divineth. Magic was widely practised in Egypt under different forms. The particular form alluded to here is hydromancy or water-divination. Into a silver cup filled with water precious metals or stones were dropped, and the future was divined from the movements of the water or the re-flexion caused by the objects. Augustine claims that the nymph Egeria, who was supposed to have given to Numa the King of Rome his laws, really stood for hydromancy.

9. The brothers are so sure of their innocence that they propose the severest punishment in case the guilt should be brought home to them.

12 sack to the ground, and opened every man his sack. And
he searched, *and* began at the eldest, and left at the
youngest: and the cup was found in Benjamin's sack.
13 Then they rent their clothes, and laded every man his ass,
14 and returned to the city. And Judah and his brethren
came to Joseph's house; and he was yet there: and they
15 fell before him on the ground. And Joseph said unto them,
What deed is this that ye have done? know ye not that
16 such a man as I can indeed divine? And Judah said, What
shall we say unto my lord? what shall we speak? or how
shall we clear ourselves? God hath found out the iniquity
of thy servants: behold, we are my lord's bondmen, both
17 we, and he also in whose hand the cup is found. And he
said, God forbid that I should do so: the man in whose
hand the cup is found, he shall be my bondman; but as
for you, get you up in peace unto your father.

18-34. *Judah's intercession.*

18 Then Judah came near unto him, and said, Oh my lord,
let thy servant, I pray thee, speak a word in my lord's ears,
and let not thine anger burn against thy servant: for thou
19 art even as Pharaoh. My lord asked his servants, saying,

---

12. left at the youngest. It was when their trial seemed
successfully over that the cup was found.

15. can indeed divine. Joseph claims to have discovered by
divination who had stolen his cup. This would increase still
further the awe with which his brethren regarded him.

16. God hath found out. The confession is very touching.
The trials which had come upon the brothers had wrought 're-
pentance with salvation' and everything is working up to the
happy climax of the story.

18-34. As a piece of writing this section is as nearly as possible
perfect. It would be difficult to improve on either the thought
or the language in which it is expressed. Judah speaks with
perfect naturalness and simplicity and with the deepest pathos,
and his offer to take Benjamin's place as a bondman shews him
as entirely unselfish. The only point in which he displays reti-
cence is as to why he believed the other brother to be dead.

Have ye a father, or a brother? And we said unto my lord, 20
We have a father, an old man, and a child of his old age,
a little one; and his brother is dead, and he alone is left
of his mother, and his father loveth him. And thou saidst 21
unto thy servants, Bring him down unto me, that I may
set mine eyes upon him. And we said unto my lord, The 22
lad cannot leave his father: for if he should leave his
father, his father would die. And thou saidst unto thy 23
servants, Except your youngest brother come down with
you, ye shall see my face no more. And it came to pass 24
when we came up unto thy servant my father, we told him
the words of my lord. And our father said, Go again, buy 25
us a little food. And we said, We cannot go down: if our 26
youngest brother be with us, then will we go down: for
we may not see the man's face, except our youngest brother
be with us. And thy servant my father said unto us, Ye 27
know that my wife bare me two sons: and the one went 28
out from me, and I said, Surely he is torn in pieces; and
I have not seen him since: and if ye take this one also 29
from me, and mischief befall him, ye shall bring down my
gray hairs with sorrow to the grave. Now therefore when 30
I come to thy servant my father, and the lad be not with
us; seeing that his life is bound up in the lad's life; it shall 31
come to pass, when he seeth that the lad is not *with us*,
that he will die: and thy servants shall bring down the
gray hairs of thy servant our father with sorrow to the
grave. For thy servant became surety for the lad unto my 32
father, saying, If I bring him not unto thee, then shall I
bear the blame to my father for ever. Now therefore, let 33

---

20. his brother is dead: more definite than 'is not' (xlii. 13).

30. his life is bound up in the lad's life. A very effective
way of expressing the thought that the loss of his son would kill
the aged father.

31. bring down the gray hairs. These were Jacob's own words,
xlii. 38.

thy servant, I pray thee, abide instead of the lad a bondman to my lord; and let the lad go up with his brethren.
34 For how shall I go up to my father, and the lad be not
with me? lest I see the evil that shall come on my father.

xlv. 1-15. *Joseph reveals himself to his brethren.*

45 Then Joseph could not refrain himself before all them
that stood by him; and he cried, Cause every man to go
out from me. And there stood no man with him, while
2 Joseph made himself known unto his brethren. And he
wept aloud: and the Egyptians heard, and the house of
3 Pharaoh heard. And Joseph said unto his brethren, I am
Joseph; doth my father yet live? And his brethren could
not answer him; for they were troubled at his presence.
4 And Joseph said unto his brethren, Come near to me, I
pray you. And they came near. And he said, I am Joseph
5 your brother, whom ye sold into Egypt. And now be not
grieved, nor angry with yourselves that ye sold me hither:
6 for God did send me before you to preserve life. For
these two years hath the famine been in the land: and there
are yet five years, in the which there shall be neither plow-
7 ing nor harvest. And God sent me before you to preserve
you a remnant in the earth, and to save you alive by a
8 great deliverance. So now it was not you that sent me
hither, but God: and he hath made me a father to Pharaoh,

---

34. lest I see the evil. The phrase (= 'to look upon') always
expresses deep emotion either of joy or grief.

xlv. 1. could not refrain himself. Judah's appeal had broken
down the last barrier of reserve.

2. he wept aloud. Cf. v. 14. This time there could be no
hiding his secret.

3. doth my father yet live? He had asked the same question
before (xliii. 27), but then it was 'your father.'

5. God did send me before you. Joseph excuses his brethren
in the only way possible by representing that their deed was the
working out of the overruling purpose of God.

8. a father to Pharaoh. This may very possibly have been an

and lord of all his house, and ruler over all the land of
Egypt. Haste ye, and go up to my father, and say unto 9
him, Thus saith thy son Joseph, God hath made me lord
of all Egypt: come down unto me, tarry not: and thou 10
shalt dwell in the land of Goshen, and thou shalt be near
unto me, thou, and thy children, and thy children's children, and thy flocks, and thy herds, and all that thou hast:
and there will I nourish thee; for there are yet five years 11
of famine; lest thou come to poverty, thou, and thy household, and all that thou hast. And, behold, your eyes see, 12
and the eyes of my brother Benjamin, that it is my mouth
that speaketh unto you. And ye shall tell my father of all 13
my glory in Egypt, and of all that ye have seen; and ye
shall haste and bring down my father hither. And he fell 14
upon his brother Benjamin's neck, and wept; and Benjamin wept upon his neck. And he kissed all his brethren, 15
and wept upon them: and after that his brethren talked
with him.

16-28. *Pharaoh sends the brethren to bring their father to Egypt.*

And the fame thereof was heard in Pharaoh's house, 16
saying, Joseph's brethren are come: and it pleased Pharaoh
well, and his servants. And Pharaoh said unto Joseph, 17
Say unto thy brethren, This do ye; lade your beasts, and

---

actual title. Compare the Roman title 'pater patriæ.' The
Turkish title Atabek, applied to a chief minister, is said to mean
'chief father.'

10. in the land of Goshen: i.e. the N.E. corner of Egypt
bounded by what is now the Suez Canal. It was advisable to keep
the Israelites separate from the Egyptians (xliii. 32). Goshen
may represent the Egyptian Kesem, the name of a district in
the Eastern Delta.

near unto me. Joseph may have been living at Avaris. See
Intr. p. 8 and xlii. 9.

15. kissed all his brethren. Shewing the reality of his forgiveness. Cf. Luke xv. 20.

18 go, get you unto the land of Canaan; and take your father
and your households, and come unto me: and I will give
you the good of the land of Egypt, and ye shall eat the fat
19 of the land. Now thou art commanded, this do ye; take
you wagons out of the land of Egypt for your little ones,
20 and for your wives, and bring your father, and come. Also
regard not your stuff; for the good of all the land of Egypt
21 is yours. And the sons of Israel did so: and Joseph gave
them wagons, according to the commandment of Pharaoh,
22 and gave them provision for the way. To all of them he
gave each man changes of raiment; but to Benjamin he
gave three hundred pieces of silver, and five changes of
23 raiment. And to his father he sent after this manner; ten
asses laden with the good things of Egypt, and ten she-
asses laden with corn and bread and victual for his father
24 by the way. So he sent his brethren away, and they departed: and he said unto them, See that ye fall not out by
25 the way. And they went up out of Egypt, and came into
26 the land of Canaan unto Jacob their father. And they told
him, saying, Joseph is yet alive, and he is ruler over all
the land of Egypt. And his heart fainted, for he believed
27 them not. And they told him all the words of Joseph,
which he had said unto them: and when he saw the
wagons which Joseph had sent to carry him, the spirit of

---

19. thou art commanded. Apparently addressed to Joseph.
The Syriac version adds 'say to thy brethren.'

wagons: the first mention of wheeled traffic in the Bible.
Egypt has never been famous for its roads, and wagons are
hardly ever seen at the present day outside the larger towns.

22. changes of raiment: i.e. best clothes for holidays and
festivals. Cf. 2 Kings v. 22, 23.

three hundred pieces of silver. Great riches for a lad.
Joseph himself had been sold for only 20 (xxxvii. 28).

24. See that ye fall not out: i.e. quarrel not. A touch of humour. The brothers had had enough of jealousy and quarrelling.

26. fainted: lit. 'became numb.' A very natural touch. But
the sight of the wagons drawn up outside dispels all doubt.

Jacob their father revived: and Israel said, It is enough; 28 Joseph my son is yet alive: I will go and see him before I die.

xlvi. 1–7. *Jacob and his household come down to Egypt.*

And Israel took his journey with all that he had, and **46** came to Beer-sheba, and offered sacrifices unto the God of his father Isaac. And God spake unto Israel in the visions 2 of the night, and said, Jacob, Jacob. And he said, Here am I. And he said, I am God, the God of thy father: fear 3 not to go down into Egypt; for I will there make of thee a great nation: I will go down with thee into Egypt; and 4 I will also surely bring thee up again: and Joseph shall put his hand upon thine eyes. And Jacob rose up from 5 Beer-sheba: and the sons of Israel carried Jacob their father, and their little ones, and their wives, in the wagons which Pharaoh had sent to carry him. And they took 6 their cattle, and their goods, which they had gotten in the land of Canaan, and came into Egypt, Jacob, and all his seed with him: his sons, and his sons' sons with him, his 7 daughters, and his sons' daughters, and all his seed brought he with him into Egypt.

---

xlvi. 1. took his journey: apparently from Hebron (xxxvii. 14).

Beer-sheba: the southernmost town and sanctuary in the land, connected especially with Isaac (xxvi. 23–25). Jacob wished to gain Divine sanction for his journey.

2. in the visions of the night: i.e. dreams. So in E God's messages are often brought, cf. xx. 3, xxxi. 24.

4. I will go down with thee. Compare the similar promise at Beth-el (xxviii. 15).

bring thee up: the words refer to the descendants of Jacob rather than to himself. It might seem that in leaving Canaan for Egypt Jacob was forfeiting the promise made to Abraham (xii. 7).

put his hand upon thine eyes: i.e. close the eyes in death.

6, 7. The reader is conscious of a change of style in these two verses which exhibit the characteristics of P.

8–27. The list of those who came to Egypt.

8 And these are the names of the children of Israel, which
came into Egypt, Jacob and his sons: Reuben, Jacob's
9 firstborn. And the sons of Reuben; Hanoch, and Pallu,
10 and Hezron, and Carmi. And the sons of Simeon; Jemuel,
and Jamin, and Ohad, and Jachin, and Zohar, and Shaul
11 the son of a Canaanitish woman. And the sons of Levi;
12 Gershon, Kohath, and Merari. And the sons of Judah;
Er, and Onan, and Shelah, and Perez, and Zerah: but Er
and Onan died in the land of Canaan. And the sons of
13 Perez were Hezron and Hamul. And the sons of Issachar;
14 Tola, and Puvah, and Iob, and Shimron. And the sons
15 of Zebulun; Sered, and Elon, and Jahleel. These are the
sons of Leah, which she bare unto Jacob in Paddan-aram,
with his daughter Dinah: all the souls of his sons and his
16 daughters were thirty and three. And the sons of Gad;
Ziphion, and Haggi, Shuni, and Ezbon, Eri, and Arodi,
17 and Areli. And the sons of Asher; Imnah, and Ishvah,
and Ishvi, and Beriah, and Serah their sister: and the
18 sons of Beriah; Heber, and Malchiel. These are the sons
of Zilpah, which Laban gave to Leah his daughter, and
19 these she bare unto Jacob, even sixteen souls. The sons
20 of Rachel Jacob's wife; Joseph and Benjamin. And unto
Joseph in the land of Egypt were born Manasseh and

8–27. Parallel lists are found in Numb. xxvi. 5–51; 1 Chron.
ii.–viii. and (in part) Exod. vi. 14–16. The list is partly arti-
ficial: e.g. the sons of Leah 32 and of her maid Zilpah 16 (i.e.
exactly half). So of Rachel 14 and Bilhah 7. And Joseph's sons
Ephraim and Manasseh are mentioned among those who 'came
into Egypt,' as well as the sons of Benjamin who was still a lad.

11. Gershon, Kohath, and Merari. The same names in Exod.
vi. 16; Numb. iii. 17; 1 Chron. vi. 1, xxiii. 6.

12. Er and Onan died: cf. xxxviii. 7, 10.

15. with his daughter Dinah. Probably an interpolation, as
Dinah is not included in the thirty-three descendants. Or it may
be that Dinah and Jacob himself are included, and Er and Onan
omitted.

Ephraim, which Asenath the daughter of Poti-phera priest
of On bare unto him. And the sons of Benjamin ; Bela, 21
and Becher, and Ashbel, Gera, and Naaman, Ehi, and
Rosh, Muppim, and Huppim, and Ard. These are 22
the sons of Rachel, which were born to Jacob : all
the souls were fourteen. And the sons of Dan ; Hushim. 23
And the sons of Naphtali ; Jahzeel, and Guni, and Jezer, 24
and Shillem. These are the sons of Bilhah, which Laban 25
gave unto Rachel his daughter, and these she bare unto
Jacob: all the souls were seven. All the souls that came 26
with Jacob into Egypt, which came out of his loins,
besides Jacob's sons' wives, all the souls were threescore
and six; and the sons of Joseph, which were born to him in 27
Egypt, were two souls : all the souls of the house of Jacob,
which came into Egypt, were threescore and ten.

28–34. *Israel and his household arrive in Goshen.*

And he sent Judah before him unto Joseph, to shew 28
the way before him unto Goshen; and they came into the
land of Goshen. And Joseph made ready his chariot, and 29
went up to meet Israel his father, to Goshen ; and he presented himself unto him, and fell on his neck, and wept
on his neck a good while. And Israel said unto Joseph, 30
Now let me die, since I have seen thy face, that thou art
yet alive. And Joseph said unto his brethren, and unto 31
his father's house, I will go up, and tell Pharaoh, and will
say unto him, My brethren, and my father's house, which
were in the land of Canaan, are come unto me ; and the 32

---

27. three score and ten. The Septuagint gives 'three score
and fifteen' and is followed in Acts vii. 14. The extra five
persons are made up of the three grandsons and two great grandsons born to Joseph in Egypt.

28. to shew the way before him. The meaning is not quite
certain. Perhaps 'to announce him beforehand.' The Septuagint
has 'he sent Judah before him to Joseph to meet him at Heroopolis
in the land of Rameses.'

30. Now let me die. It was Jacob's *Nunc Dimittis*.

men are shepherds, for they have been keepers of cattle;
and they have brought their flocks, and their herds, and
33 all that they have. And it shall come to pass, when Pharaoh shall call you, and shall say, What is your occupation?
34 that ye shall say, Thy servants have been keepers of cattle
from our youth even until now, both we, and our fathers:
that ye may dwell in the land of Goshen; for every shepherd is an abomination unto the Egyptians.

> xlvii. 1-12. *Jacob and his sons are settled in the
> land of Goshen.*

47   Then Joseph went in and told Pharaoh, and said, My
father and my brethren, and their flocks, and their herds,
and all that they have, are come out of the land of Canaan;
2 and, behold, they are in the land of Goshen. And from
among his brethren he took five men, and presented them
3 unto Pharaoh. And Pharaoh said unto his brethren, What
is your occupation? And they said unto Pharaoh, Thy
4 servants are shepherds, both we, and our fathers. And
they said unto Pharaoh, To sojourn in the land are we
come; for there is no pasture for thy servants' flocks; for
the famine is sore in the land of Canaan: now therefore,
we pray thee, let thy servants dwell in the land of Goshen.
5 And Pharaoh spake unto Joseph, saying, Thy father and
6 thy brethren are come unto thee: the land of Egypt is

---

32. shepherds...keepers of cattle. The two expressions seem
to be used with the same meaning.

34. every shepherd is an abomination. The statement seems
too sweeping, for the Egyptians too kept sheep. But the nomads
of the desert who lived by pasturing flocks were always objects
of suspicion to them. If however the Hyksos were in power at
this time, the note seems out of place. See Introduction, p. 8.

xlvii. 2. five men. For the number five in connection with
Egypt cf. xli. 34, xliii. 34, xlv. 22.

5. Pharaoh spake unto Joseph. The brothers are sent away
after making their request, and Pharaoh's answer is communicated
through Joseph.

before thee; in the best of the land make thy father and
thy brethren to dwell; in the land of Goshen let them
dwell: and if thou knowest any able men among them,
then make them rulers over my cattle. And Joseph brought 7
in Jacob his father, and set him before Pharaoh: and
Jacob blessed Pharaoh. And Pharaoh said unto Jacob, 8
How many are the days of the years of thy life? And 9
Jacob said unto Pharaoh, The days of the years of my
pilgrimage are an hundred and thirty years: few and evil
have been the days of the years of my life, and they have
not attained unto the days of the years of the life of my
fathers in the days of their pilgrimage. And Jacob blessed 10
Pharaoh, and went out from the presence of Pharaoh.
And Joseph placed his father and his brethren, and gave 11
them a possession in the land of Egypt, in the best of the
land, in the land of Rameses, as Pharaoh had commanded. And Joseph nourished his father, and his brethren, 12
and all his father's household, with bread, according to
their families.

13–27. *The Egyptians pledge all that they have for corn.*

And there was no bread in all the land; for the famine 13

---

6. over my cattle. The inscriptions shew that the Egyptians
paid great attention to cattle rearing.

7. blessed Pharaoh: or perhaps 'saluted' for the 'less is
blessed of the greater.' But it may have been an old man's
privilege to bless.

9. pilgrimage: better with R.V. marg. *sojournings* for Jacob
had known little of any fixed home. For the metaphorical idea
of pilgrimage cf. Hebr. xi. 13; 2 Pet. ii. 11.

few and evil. Abraham had lived to be 175 (xxv. 7) and Isaac
180 (xxxv. 28). Looking back over his life it seems to Jacob that
the evil has overweighed the good in it.

11. the land of Rameses. Rameses is identified with Tel-el-
Mashkuta some 12 miles W. of Ismailia. But the town itself was
built by Rameses II long after this time.

13. in all the land: or, perhaps, ' in all the world': cf. Acts
xi. 28.

was very sore, so that the land of Egypt and the land of
14 Canaan fainted by reason of the famine. And Joseph
gathered up all the money that was found in the land of
Egypt, and in the land of Canaan, for the corn which they
bought: and Joseph brought the money into Pharaoh's
15 house. And when the money was all spent in the land of
Egypt, and in the land of Canaan, all the Egyptians came
unto Joseph, and said, Give us bread: for why should we
16 die in thy presence? for *our* money faileth. And Joseph
said, Give your cattle; and I will give you for your cattle,
17 if money fail. And they brought their cattle unto Joseph:
and Joseph gave them bread in exchange for the horses,
and for the flocks, and for the herds, and for the asses:
and he fed them with bread in exchange for all their cattle
18 for that year. And when that year was ended, they came
unto him the second year, and said unto him, We will not
hide from my lord, how that our money is all spent; and
the herds of cattle are my lord's; there is nought left in
19 the sight of my lord, but our bodies, and our lands: wherefore should we die before thine eyes, both we and our land?
buy us and our land for bread, and we and our land will
be servants unto Pharaoh: and give us seed, that we may
20 live, and not die, and that the land be not desolate. So
Joseph bought all the land of Egypt for Pharaoh; for the

---

14. into Pharaoh's house. The revenue is regarded as Pharaoh's absolute property.

17. the horses. It is said that horses were first introduced
into Egypt in the time of the Hyksos kings. In Solomon's time
they became one of the regular exports from Egypt: 1 Kings x.
28.

We are perhaps not to understand the verse literally, for it is
hardly to be imagined that all the cattle of Egypt were gathered
together in one place. What is meant is that they became
Pharaoh's property.

19. buy us and our land. The attitude of the people is re-
markable: there are no riots, and they appear to acquiesce
cheerfully in the loss of all their land and property.

Egyptians sold every man his field, because the famine
was sore upon them: and the land became Pharaoh's.
And as for the people, he removed them to the cities from 21
one end of the border of Egypt even to the other end
thereof. Only the land of the priests bought he not: for 22
the priests had a portion from Pharaoh, and did eat their
portion which Pharaoh gave them; wherefore they sold
not their land. Then Joseph said unto the people, Behold, 23
I have bought you this day and your land for Pharaoh:
lo, here is seed for you, and ye shall sow the land. And 24
it shall come to pass at the ingatherings, that ye shall give
a fifth unto Pharaoh, and four parts shall be your own, for
seed of the field, and for your food, and for them of your
households, and for food for your little ones. And they 25
said, Thou hast saved our lives: let us find grace in the
sight of my lord, and we will be Pharaoh's servants. And 26
Joseph made it a statute concerning the land of Egypt
unto this day, that Pharaoh should have the fifth; only
the land of the priests alone became not Pharaoh's. And 27

---

21. he removed them to the cities. If the reading is right it
must have been a temporary measure to facilitate the feeding of
the people. But several Versions read 'he made bondmen of
them according to the cities': this involves only the smallest
alteration of the Hebrew text, and is probably correct.

22. the land of the priests. Apparently the priests enjoyed
a regular provision of food, and therefore they did not feel the
famine. An inscription of Rameses III says that 185,000 sacks
of corn were given yearly to the temples.

23. ye shall sow the land. The seven years of famine are
at last at an end.

24. a fifth. An income tax of 4s. in the £ does not seem so
much now as it did a few years ago: and the Egyptians seem to
have accepted it with gratitude (*v.* 25).

26. unto this day. The system appears to have obtained when
the account was written. There are traces of it preserved in the
inscriptions. Whereas in the early dynasties large estates were
owned by the nobility, in the 15th and following dynasties the
land seems to have passed into the possession of the Crown and
of the great Temples.

Israel dwelt in the land of Egypt, in the land of Goshen;
and they gat them possessions therein, and were fruitful,
and multiplied exceedingly.

28–31. *Jacob enjoins on Joseph to bury him in Canaan.*

28 And Jacob lived in the land of Egypt seventeen years:
so the days of Jacob, the years of his life, were an hundred
29 forty and seven years. And the time drew near that Israel
must die: and he called his son Joseph, and said unto
him, If now I have found grace in thy sight, put, I pray
thee, thy hand under my thigh, and deal kindly and truly
30 with me; bury me not, I pray thee, in Egypt: but when I
sleep with my fathers, thou shalt carry me out of Egypt,
and bury me in their buryingplace. And he said, I will do
31 as thou hast said. And he said, Swear unto me: and he
sware unto him. And Israel bowed himself upon the bed's
head.

xlviii. *Jacob blesses Ephraim and Manasseh.*

48 And it came to pass after these things, that one said to
Joseph, Behold, thy father is sick: and he took with him
2 his two sons, Manasseh and Ephraim. And one told Jacob,
and said, Behold, thy son Joseph cometh unto thee: and

---

27. Israel. Here, as in xxxiv. 7, used for the people as dis-
tinguished from the individual.

were fruitful: i.e. when prosperity returned to the land.

29. put...thy hand under my thigh: i.e. to pledge not only
himself but also his descendants (cf. xxiv. 2 with note).

deal kindly and truly: cf. xxiv. 49; Josh. ii. 14.

30. in their buryingplace: i.e. in the cave of Machpelah: cf.
l. 13. Here Abraham was buried (xxv. 9) and Isaac (xxxv. 29).

31. Israel bowed himself: probably in silent thanksgiving to
God, cf. 1 Kings i. 47. He was too feeble to get up and pro-
strate himself on the ground.

upon the bed's head. The quotation in Hebr. xi. 21 'and
worshipped leaning upon the top of his staff' comes from the
LXX here. It is a rendering of the same consonantal text, pointed
with different vowels.

Israel strengthened himself, and sat upon the bed. And 3
Jacob said unto Joseph, God Almighty appeared unto me
at Luz in the land of Canaan, and blessed me, and said 4
unto me, Behold, I will make thee fruitful, and multiply
thee, and I will make of thee a company of peoples; and
will give this land to thy seed after thee for an everlasting
possession. And now thy two sons, which were born unto 5
thee in the land of Egypt before I came unto thee into
Egypt, are mine; Ephraim and Manasseh, even as Reuben and Simeon, shall be mine. And thy issue, which thou 6
begettest after them, shall be thine; they shall be called
after the name of their brethren in their inheritance. And 7
as for me, when I came from Paddan, Rachel died by me
in the land of Canaan in the way, when there was still
some way to come unto Ephrath: and I buried her there
in the way to Ephrath (the same is Beth-lehem). And 8
Israel beheld Joseph's sons, and said, Who are these?
And Joseph said unto his father, They are my sons, whom 9
God hath given me here. And he said, Bring them, I pray
thee, unto me, and I will bless them. Now the eyes of 10
Israel were dim for age, so that he could not see. And he
brought them near unto him; and he kissed them, and
embraced them. And Israel said unto Joseph, I had not 11
thought to see thy face: and, lo, God hath let me see thy

---

xlviii. 3. **God Almighty appeared unto me.** Jacob's thoughts
go back to God's first promise to him at Beth-el.

5. **Ephraim and Manasseh.** In Jacob's prophetic mind
Ephraim comes first. Contrast *v.* 1.

7. **from Paddan.** Paddan = Paddan-aram, P's name for Mesopotamia. The whole passage, *vv.* 3-7, is from P and the references
are to P's account in xxxv. 11, 16 ff.

died by me: lit. '[as a weight] upon me,' i.e. to my sorrow.

Ephrath (the same is Beth-lehem). See note on xxxv. 19.

10. **were dim for age:** like those of his father Isaac (xxvii. 1).
Like Isaac too he blessed the younger before the elder, but not
through any fraud practised upon him.

12 seed also. And Joseph brought them out from between
his knees; and he bowed himself with his face to the
13 earth. And Joseph took them both, Ephraim in his
right hand toward Israel's left hand, and Manasseh in
his left hand toward Israel's right hand, and brought
14 them near unto him. And Israel stretched out his right
hand, and laid it upon Ephraim's head, who was the
younger, and his left hand upon Manasseh's head, guiding
his hands wittingly; for Manasseh was the firstborn.
15 And he blessed Joseph, and said, The God before whom
my fathers Abraham and Isaac did walk, the God which
16 hath fed me all my life long unto this day, the angel
which hath redeemed me from all evil, bless the lads;
and let my name be named on them, and the name of my
fathers Abraham and Isaac: and let them grow into a
17 multitude in the midst of the earth. And when Joseph
saw that his father laid his right hand upon the head of
Ephraim, it displeased him: and he held up his father's
hand, to remove it from Ephraim's head unto Manasseh's

---

12. brought them...from between his knees. A father took an
infant upon his knees to signify that he recognized him as his
own son. So apparently Jacob had Ephraim and Manasseh put
between his knees to signify that he adopted the lads into his
family and reckoned them as his sons.

he bowed himself. The subject may be either Jacob or Joseph,
and the act was an act of thanksgiving.

14. guiding his hands wittingly. The verb may mean, as in
Arabic, 'crossing his hands.' So LXX and R.V. marg. Either
makes good sense.

15. before whom...did walk. An expressive phrase for life-
long service: cf. xvii. 1.

16. the angel: apparently = God as He appears to men.

hath redeemed me: the verb is usually used technically of the
duties performed by the next of kin. Here as in Job xix. 25 it
has a more general sense.

17. he held up his father's hand. This verse should logically
come before vv. 15, 16. It is misplaced to avoid breaking the
sequence, cf. vv. 14–16.

head. And Joseph said unto his father, Not so, my father: 18
for this is the firstborn; put thy right hand upon his head.
And his father refused, and said, I know *it*, my son, I 19
know *it*: he also shall become a people, and he also shall
be great: howbeit his younger brother shall be greater
than he, and his seed shall become a multitude of nations.
And he blessed them that day, saying, In thee shall Israel 20
bless, saying, God make thee as Ephraim and as Manasseh:
and he set Ephraim before Manasseh. And Israel said 21
unto Joseph, Behold, I die: but God shall be with you,
and bring you again unto the land of your fathers. More- 22
over I have given to thee one portion above thy brethren,
which I took out of the hand of the Amorite with my
sword and with my bow.

xlix. 1–28. *Jacob's Blessing.*

And Jacob called unto his sons, and said: Gather your- 49

---

19. his younger brother shall be greater. In Numb. xxvi.
34, 37 Manasseh is more numerous than Ephraim. But from the
time of the Judges Ephraim became the most powerful tribe.

20. In thee shall Israel bless: i.e. Israel shall quote thee as
a type of those whom God hath blessed. The same thought may
underlie the words ' In thee shall all the families of the earth be
blessed,' xii. 3, etc.

22. one portion: lit. 'one shoulder.' The Hebrew word for
' shoulder' is *shechem* which seems to allude to Shechem
(=? mountain slope) being included in the territory of Ephraim.

which I took. Genesis has no other allusion to this. In xxxiii.
19 Jacob purchases a 'parcel of ground' from the children of
Hamor, Shechem's father. In xxxiv. the sons of Jacob massacre
the Shechemites, but Jacob has no part in this, and expressly
condemns it. There was probably a tradition of a conquest of
Shechem by Jacob and his family, and indeed such an expedition
is mentioned in the Book of Jubilees, a Rabbinic paraphrase of
Genesis.

the Amorite. A name for the ancient inhabitants of Palestine,
cf. x. 16, xv. 16; Amos ii. 9.

with my sword and with my bow. There is a curious substitute
in the Targum of Onkelos, 'with my prayer and entreaty.'

xlix. The above title of this chapter is perhaps the most con-

selves together, that I may tell you that which shall befall you in the latter days.

2   Assemble yourselves, and hear, ye sons of Jacob;
    And hearken unto Israel your father.

3   Reuben, thou art my firstborn, my might, and the
        beginning of my strength;
    The excellency of dignity, and the excellency of power.

4   Unstable as water, thou shalt not have the excellency;
    Because thou wentest up to thy father's bed:
    Then defiledst thou it: he went up to my couch.

5   Simeon and Levi are brethren;

---

venient, although it is not strictly accurate. Only two tribes (Judah and Joseph) are actually blessed, while two (Simeon and Levi) receive a curse. It is rather a prediction of the fortunes and geographical position of the several tribes, and as such it is to be compared with Isaac's Blessing on Jacob and Esau as related in xxvii., and more closely with the Blessing of Moses in Deut. xxxiii. In all these cases we have to make up our minds whether the passages are genuine prophecies foretelling with accuracy events that should happen many years later, or whether they are descriptions of existing conditions put in the mouth of some prominent man long since dead. A study of the nature of Old Testament prophecy inclines us to the latter view. If this is correct Jacob's Blessing is a vivid portrait of the main characteristics, geographical or racial, of the various tribes soon after they had settled down in the Promised Land.

The tribes are mentioned in the following order. First the six sons of Leah, then Dan, Bilhah's eldest son, then the sons of Zilpah, then Bilhah's other son, and finally the two sons of Rachel.

1. in the latter days. The expression, occurring 14 times in the O.T., is almost a technical one and seems to denote the end of the period of the future with which the writer is dealing.

3, 4. Reuben's proud position as the eldest son is ruined by his moral character. No man of eminence is recorded as belonging to this tribe.

3. the excellency: i.e. the pre-eminence.

4. Unstable. The literal meaning is 'bubbling.' The same word in Judg. ix. 4 is rendered 'light,' i.e. 'reckless.'

thou wentest up: referring to xxxv. 22.

Weapons of violence are their swords.

O my soul, come not thou into their council;   6

Unto their assembly, my glory, be not thou united;

For in their anger they slew a man,

And in their selfwill they houghed an ox.

Cursed be their anger, for it was fierce;   7

And their wrath, for it was cruel:

I will divide them in Jacob,

And scatter them in Israel.

   Judah, thee shall thy brethren praise: 8

Thy hand shall be on the neck of thine enemies;

Thy father's sons shall bow down before thee.

Judah is a lion's whelp;   9

From the prey, my son, thou art gone up:

He stooped down, he crouched as a lion,

And as a lioness; who shall rouse him up?

The sceptre shall not depart from Judah,   10

5–7. Simeon and Levi coupled together. They are upbraided for their massacre of the Shechemites, xxxiv. 25, 30.

5. their swords. The meaning of the word is uncertain. Perhaps 'marriage-contracts' or 'plots.'

6. my glory: parallel to 'my soul' and meaning the same thing. Cf. Ps. xvi. 9.

houghed: i.e. 'mutilated' by cutting the sinews of the leg. Cf. Josh. xi. 6, 9; 2 Sam. viii. 4 (of disabling a horse). The word is pronounced *hock*, and appears in Old English as *hox*. There is no special mention of this form of outrage in ch. xxxiv.

7. I will divide them. The Levites were scattered among the other tribes with no territory of their own, and Simeon virtually disappeared as a tribe, being ultimately merged with Judah.

8–12. Judah. This tribe, together with Joseph, receives a special blessing corresponding to its importance in later history.

8. praise. Judah means 'praise.' Cf. xxix. 35.

Thy father's sons shall bow down: cf. xxvii. 29.

9. a lion's whelp: cf. Rev. v. 5 'the Lion of the tribe of Judah.' The same simile is applied to Gad (Deut. xxxiii. 20) and to Dan (Deut. xxxiii. 22).

10. The sceptre. Probably the royal sceptre, though it might be the staff or baton of a general.

Nor the ruler's staff from between his feet,
Until Shiloh come;
And unto him shall the obedience of the peoples be.

11 Binding his foal unto the vine,
And his ass's colt unto the choice vine;
He hath washed his garments in wine,
And his vesture in the blood of grapes:

12 His eyes shall be red with wine,
And his teeth white with milk.

13   Zebulun shall dwell at the haven of the sea:
And he shall be for an haven of ships;
And his border shall be upon Zidon.

14   Issachar is a strong ass,

---

the ruler's staff: the wand of the judge, which he holds between his legs as the symbol of office.

Until Shiloh come. A much disputed sentence. Three explanations may be noted: (i) R.V. text takes Shiloh as a proper name (perhaps = Peaceful). This is understood as a name of Messiah, but it rests on nothing earlier than a fanciful passage in the Talmud. (ii) R.V. marg. (1) 'Till he come to Shiloh.' Shiloh was the place where the ark rested in the centre of the tribe of Ephraim, 1 Sam. i. 24. But it is difficult to see why this should be taken as a turning point in Judah's sovereignty. (iii) R.V. marg. (2) 'Till he come whose it is,' i.e. the sceptre and staff. 'He whose it is' might be a paraphrase for Messiah. This explanation seems on the whole the least unlikely.

11. Binding his foal. The verse expresses the fertility of the territory of Judah.

the blood of grapes. A poetic synonym for wine, cf. Deut. xxxii. 14.

12. red: perhaps 'sparkling.' But the word is only found again in Prov. xxiii. 29 where it refers to redness from excessive drinking.

white with milk. For 'milk' as emblem of whiteness cf. Lam. iv. 7; Song of Songs v. 12.

13. Zebulun.

haven: better 'shore.' Zebulun's territory as defined in Josh. xix. 10–16 was entirely inland, but Josephus says that it touched the sea ('that which belongeth to Carmel and the sea').

14. Issachar.

a strong ass: i.e. content to be a well-fed beast of burden.

Couching down between the sheepfolds:

And he saw a resting place that it was good,   15

And the land that it was pleasant;

And he bowed his shoulder to bear,

And became a servant under taskwork.

    Dan shall judge his people,   16

As one of the tribes of Israel.

Dan shall be a serpent in the way,   17

An adder in the path,

That biteth the horse's heels,

So that his rider falleth backward.

I have waited for thy salvation, O LORD.   18

    Gad, a troop shall press upon him: 19

But he shall press upon their heel.

    Out of Asher his bread shall be fat,   20

---

between the sheepfolds: the same word in Judg. v. 16; Ps. lxviii. 13, giving in each case a picture of ignoble ease. But the meaning is not quite certain, and Skinner suggests here 'between the panniers' which would suit well the picture of an ass of burden.

15. a servant under taskwork: cf. Deut. xx. 11; Josh. xvi. 10. Taskwork means enforced and unpaid labour, like the corvée, and always implies a condition of servitude.

16, 17. Dan.

shall judge. Another play on names as in *v*. 8. Dan means 'judge.'

As one of the tribes: i.e. as an independent tribe in spite of being always small in numbers.

17. a serpent in the way. Dan apparently gained a reputation for resourcefulness in guerilla warfare. Compare the story in Judg. xviii.

18. An interjection. Possibly Jacob pauses a moment from physical weakness.

19. Gad.

a troop shall press. A double play on words. Gad is represented as shaking off a heavy attack and inflicting a blow on the retiring foe. There may be a reference to Jephthah's victory over Ammon, Judg. xi.

20. Asher.

Out of Asher. The letter representing 'out of' really belongs

And he shall yield royal dainties.

21   Naphtali is a hind let loose :
He giveth goodly words.

22   Joseph is a fruitful bough,
A fruitful bough by a fountain ;
His branches run over the wall.

23   The archers have sorely grieved him,
And shot at him, and persecuted him :

24   But his bow abode in strength,
And the arms of his hands were made strong,
By the hands of the Mighty One of Jacob,
(From thence is the shepherd, the stone of Israel,)

---

to the last word of *v.* 19 (their heel). So R.V. marg. is right :
Asher, his bread shall be fat. Asher's territory lay along the
sea from Carmel to Phœnicia, and was rich and fertile.

21. Naphtali.

a hind let loose: i.e. exulting in the freedom of the mountains
of Upper Galilee where the territory of this tribe was situated.
But the second clause does not yield a very satisfactory sense and
the verse might be rendered 'Naphtali is a slender terebinth,
putting forth beautiful top branches.'

22–26. Joseph.

Joseph, represented by the tribes of Ephraim and Manasseh,
was the most powerful and influential of the tribes.

22. fruitful bough. A play on Ephraim which means 'fruitful' (xli. 52).

run over the wall: i.e. the territory becomes too small.
Manasseh occupied land on both sides of Jordan.

23. The archers: lit. 'lords of arrows.' The reference would
be to the attacks of such foes as the Canaanites (Josh. xvii. 16) or
the Midianites (Judg. vii.).

24. in strength. The word is properly used of a constant,
never-failing stream, cf. Deut. xxi. 4; and then of anything firm
and enduring, Jer. xlix. 19.

the Mighty One of Jacob: a title that sounds a little curious
in Jacob's own mouth : cf. Ps. cxxxii. 2, 5; Isa. i. 24.

From thence…Israel. A difficult and probably corrupt line.
'Shepherd' and 'stone of Israel' are apparently titles for God.
God is sometimes called the Rock, Deut. xxxii. 4; 2 Sam. xxii. 2,
etc. but not elsewhere the Stone. There may possibly be a refer-

Even by the God of thy father, who shall help thee,   25
And by the Almighty, who shall bless thee,
With blessings of heaven above,
Blessings of the deep that coucheth beneath,
Blessings of the breasts, and of the womb.
The blessings of thy father   26
Have prevailed above the blessings of my progenitors
Unto the utmost bound of the everlasting hills:
They shall be on the head of Joseph,
And on the crown of the head of him that was separate
     from his brethren.

   Benjamin is a wolf that ravineth: 27
In the morning he shall devour the prey,
And at even he shall divide the spoil.

All these are the twelve tribes of Israel: and this is it 28
that their father spake unto them and blessed them; every
one according to his blessing he blessed them.

29–33. *Jacob's instructions as to his burial.*

And he charged them, and said unto them, I am to be 29
gathered unto my people: bury me with my fathers in the

---

ence to Ebenezer = stone of help (1 Sam. vii. 12) if the date of
the Blessing is to be placed as late as that.

25. blessings of heaven: i.e. sunshine, rain and dew.

of the deep: i.e. wells and springs.

26. A difficult verse. The word rendered 'my progenitors' is
very doubtful. A very slight emendation gives the sense 'The
blessings of thy father are mightier than the blessings of the per-
petual mountains, the desire of the everlasting hills.' This would
refer to the permanence of the blessings.

separate from his brethren: rather 'the prince of his brethren.'

27. Benjamin.
Benjamin though a small tribe was always noted for its prowess
in war. Saul the King and Saul the Apostle both belonged to
this tribe.

ravineth. An Old English word meaning to 'prey upon.'

29–33. The section comes from P and is parallel to xlvii.
28–31 (J).

30 cave that is in the field of Ephron the Hittite, in the cave
   that is in the field of Machpelah, which is before Mamre,
   in the land of Canaan, which Abraham bought with the
   field from Ephron the Hittite for a possession of a burying-
31 place: there they buried Abraham and Sarah his wife;
   there they buried Isaac and Rebekah his wife; and there
32 I buried Leah: the field and the cave that is therein, which
33 was purchased from the children of Heth. And when Jacob
   made an end of charging his sons, he gathered up his feet
   into the bed, and yielded up the ghost, and was gathered
   unto his people.

l. 1–13. *The burial of Jacob.*

50 And Joseph fell upon his father's face, and wept upon
 2 him, and kissed him. And Joseph commanded his servants
   the physicians to embalm his father: and the physicians
 3 embalmed Israel. And forty days were fulfilled for him; for
   so are fulfilled the days of embalming: and the Egyptians
   wept for him threescore and ten days.
 4   And when the days of weeping for him were past, Joseph
   spake unto the house of Pharaoh, saying, If now I have

---

31. they buried Abraham: cf. xxv. 9, 10. For Sarah's burial
cf. xxiii. 19, and for Isaac's xxxv. 29.

33. gathered up his feet: i.e. lay down on his bed.

was gathered unto his people: a characteristic phrase of P
(cf. xxv. 8) indicating some faint belief in conscious reunion after
death.

1. 2. the physicians: lit. 'the curers,' but the word is used
here, much as 'to cure' in English, in the sense of embalming.

to embalm. As the numerous mummies testify the Egyptians
were past masters in the art of embalming. 'Mummy' is an
Arabic word meaning 'bitumenized [object].' Of all ancient
peoples the Egyptians had the strongest belief in a life after
death.

3. forty days. Herodotus says that the process lasted seventy
days.

4. the house of Pharaoh. Joseph as a mourner would not
approach the king in person.

found grace in your eyes, speak, I pray you, in the ears of
Pharaoh, saying, My father made me swear, saying, Lo, I 5
die: in my grave which I have digged for me in the land
of Canaan, there shalt thou bury me. Now therefore let
me go up, I pray thee, and bury my father, and I will come
again. And Pharaoh said, Go up, and bury thy father, 6
according as he made thee swear. And Joseph went up 7
to bury his father: and with him went up all the servants
of Pharaoh, the elders of his house, and all the elders of
the land of Egypt, and all the house of Joseph, and his 8
brethren, and his father's house : only their little ones, and
their flocks, and their herds, they left in the land of Goshen.
And there went up with him both chariots and horsemen : 9
and it was a very great company. And they came to the 10
threshing-floor of Atad, which is beyond Jordan, and there
they lamented with a very great and sore lamentation:
and he made a mourning for his father seven days. And 11
when the inhabitants of the land, the Canaanites, saw the
mourning in the floor of Atad, they said, This is a grievous
mourning to the Egyptians : wherefore the name of it was
called Abel-mizraim, which is beyond Jordan. And his 12
sons did unto him according as he commanded them : for 13
his sons carried him into the land of Canaan, and buried

---

5. digged. So the LXX. But R.V. marg. *bought* is a possible meaning of the word (cf. Deut. ii. 6), and is to be preferred.

7. all the servants of Pharaoh. A mark to indicate the great
honour in which Joseph was held.

10. Atad : the word means 'bramble' and may not be a proper
name.

beyond Jordan : should mean 'east of Jordan,' but it is diffi-
cult to see why they should have gone there. It is suggested that
Jordan is a false gloss on 'the river' which would mean the
'River of Egypt' modern Wady el Arish, between Egypt and
Palestine.

11. Abel-mizraim : would mean 'meadow of Egypt' rather
than 'mourning (*ébel*) of Egypt,' but popular etymology is often
incorrect.

him in the cave of the field of Machpelah, which Abraham bought with the field, for a possession of a buryingplace, of Ephron the Hittite, before Mamre.

14-21. *Joseph reassures his brethren.*

14 And Joseph returned into Egypt, he, and his brethren, and all that went up with him to bury his father, after he 15 had buried his father. And when Joseph's brethren saw that their father was dead, they said, It may be that Joseph will hate us, and will fully requite us all the evil which we 16 did unto him. And they sent a message unto Joseph, saying, 17 Thy father did command before he died, saying, So shall ye say unto Joseph, Forgive, I pray thee now, the transgression of thy brethren, and their sin, for that they did unto thee evil: and now, we pray thee, forgive the transgression of the servants of the God of thy father. And 18 Joseph wept when they spake unto him. And his brethren also went and fell down before his face; and they 19 said, Behold, we be thy servants. And Joseph said unto 20 them, Fear not: for am I in the place of God? And as for you, ye meant evil against me; but God meant it for good, to bring to pass, as it is this day, to save much people 21 alive. Now therefore fear ye not: I will nourish you, and your little ones. And he comforted them, and spake kindly unto them.

22-26. *Joseph's death.*

22 And Joseph dwelt in Egypt, he, and his father's house:

---

15. requite us all the evil. As Esau had planned to do to his brother after their father was dead (xxvii. 41).

16. Thy father did command. Joseph's love for his father is often emphasized, and this plea of the brethren would have the strongest effect.

17. Joseph wept: cf. xlii. 24, xliii. 30, xlv. 14, 15.

19. am I in the place of God? i.e. God alone has the right to avenge or punish where necessary, cf. Ps. xciv. 1; Deut. xxxii. 35. The words occur with a somewhat different meaning in xxx. 2; 2 Kings v. 7.

20. God meant it for good: cf. xlv. 5.

and Joseph lived an hundred and ten years. And Joseph 23
saw Ephraim's children of the third generation : the children also of Machir the son of Manasseh were born upon
Joseph's knees. And Joseph said unto his brethren, I die : 24
but God will surely visit you, and bring you up out of this
land unto the land which he sware to Abraham, to Isaac,
and to Jacob. And Joseph took an oath of the children of 25
Israel, saying, God will surely visit you, and ye shall carry
up my bones from hence. So Joseph died, being an hun- 26
dred and ten years old : and they embalmed him, and he
was put in a coffin in Egypt.

---

22. an hundred and ten years. This seems to have been regarded by the Egyptians as the ideal length of life,—long enough
but not too long.

23. upon Joseph's knees. The phrase denotes that he acknowledged them as belonging to his family, cf. xxx. 3, xlviii.
12.

24. unto his brethren: probably not his own brothers who
were nearly all older than he, but to the members of his family.

26. a coffin : i.e. a sarcophagus or outer case in which the box
containing the actual mummy was enclosed.

INDEX

For EU product safety concerns, contact us at Calle de José Abascal, 56–1°, 28003 Madrid, Spain or eugpsr@cambridge.org.

www.ingramcontent.com/pod-product-compliance
Ingram Content Group UK Ltd.
Pitfield, Milton Keynes, MK11 3LW, UK
UKHW020311140625
459647UK00018B/1826